THE COMPLETE

NINJA MAX XL AIR FRYER COOKBOOK

EASY AND AFFORDABLE RECIPES TO FRY THE BEST MEALS WITH YOUR NINJA MAX XL AIR FRYER

FRED PHILLIPS

CONTENTS

INTRODUCTION

How air frying works

Have you ever seen one of those money machines, where someone steps inside a cylinder, closes the door, and air starts flowing up from the bottom with money flying through the air?

An air fryer is kind of like one of those money machines. When you put your food into the air fryer and close it, hot air circulates around the food and begins to cook it. The temperature of the air fryer and the type of food you're cooking will help determine the amount of time you need to cook your recipe.

The big difference between air frying and traditional deep frying is that air fryers require minimal to no oil to cook the food. The hot air circulating around the food helps to impart that crisp texture instead of the oil involved in deep frying.

A few other technologically advanced mechanisms are involved, but this is the gist of how air frying works. If you're familiar with convection ovens, where hot air is circulated (as opposed to conventional ovens, where the heating element is on the bottom), you'll feel right at home with air frying. An air fryer is essentially a compact convection oven.

If you want to get a bit more science based, what's actually happening from a chemical perspective when food is cooked in an air fryer is something called the Maillard reaction. The Maillard reaction is often referred to as "non-enzymatic browning," or basically a reaction that happens between sugars and amino acids in a recipe that result in the end product taking on a new flavor, texture, and color.

Seeing the benefits of air frying

Air frying is not only a healthier way to cook some more decadent recipes, but it's also efficient. Many popular models of air fryers claim that using an air fryer instead of a deep fryer can lower the fat of the dish by over 75 percent. This actually makes sense when you think about. Let's say you're going to make homemade fried chicken. If you were to use the deep-frying method of cooking, you'd traditionally need more than 3 cups of oil to cover the chicken to allow the cooking to ensue. On the other hand, if you were to use the air frying method, you'd need less than a tablespoon of oil.

Here are a few other benefits of air frying:

- **Air fryers can promote weight loss (for certain individuals).**

For individuals who currently have a highly processed diet filled with deep-fried foods, switching to air frying will certainly help with reducing caloric intake. A reduction in caloric intake will inevitably result in weight loss.

- **Air fryers can increase consumption of healthy foods, like fish, shrimp, and produce.**

Eating seafood at least twice a week, as well as increasing your consumption of fruits and vegetables, is highly recommended. If you struggle with getting your family to eat more of these foods on a regular basis, then air frying may be the best way to change their appetites (and minds!).

Not only can you put a light crunchy coating of heart-healthy nuts on some of your fried seafood favorites and cook them in the air fryer, but you can do the same with new herbs, spices, and vegetables! This is a great way to explore new vegetables and flavors in your kitchen, too.

- **Air fryers are safer (for the most part) than deep fryers.**

Deep frying can cause splatters of exceptionally hot oil all over your kitchen. Air fryers get super-hot as well, but they don't splatter in the same way a deep fryer does.

As long as you practice important safety measures when taking foods in and out of your fryer (for example, don't put your hands on the fryer basket), you can feel secure in using your fryer.

- **Air fryers can reduce the risk of potentially harmful agents on certain foods.**

A compound called *acrylamide* naturally forms on carbohydrate-rich foods (those traditionally deep-fried foods like french fries, breaded meats, and so on) when cooked at high temperatures. Some studies have found an association between acrylamide and cancer. The jury's still out on whether acrylamide actually *causes* cancer. What you need to know is that air frying is associated with a *decreased* amount of this compound as compared to deep frying, but some may still be present. We firmly believe in balance and moderation. We wouldn't recommend you eat french fries (even air-fried ones) daily.

- **Air fryers can reduce the risk of preventable diseases affected by diet and nutrition.**

This varies depending on many factors like your genetics and current lifestyle habits (such as nutrition and exercise). That said, if your diet is heavy in processed, fried foods, the air fryer may just be the ticket to enjoying the foods you crave in a new, exciting, and healthier way. Not only can you modify the amount of sodium in your recipes and use more fresh herbs and spices to give flavor to the food instead of salt, but you can also increase the fiber in your diet while including more plants in your meal plan.

Using Your Ninja Max XL Air Fryer

Each make and model of air fryer has its own instructions, but air fryers don't require extensive knowledge to operate. We recommend that you start by reading the manual that came with your Ninja Max XL air fryer and getting to know your particular machine.

With that said, here are a few basic steps that work for Your Ninja Max XL Air Fryer:

1. Clean the air fryer basket and accessories with hot soapy water and dry with a dish towel before use.
2. Plug in your air fryer and preheat it.

   This allows the machine time to get to temperature before you actually put the recipe inside.
3. Select Air Fry as the function.
4. Place your food on the wire rack or trivet, securely seal or close the drawer, and begin to air fry.
5. Check the food as applicable, following the recipe instructions.
6. When cooking completes, press Cancel and unplug the air fryer.

Caring for Your Ninja Max XL Air Fryer

You don't have to invest in any specific detergent or cleanser to keep your Ninja Max XL air fryer smelling like new. Use this section as your guide to keep your new kitchen appliance in tip-top shape so you can use it for years to come. Cleaning your Ninja Max XL air fryer is actually a really simple task. With a little elbow grease, some regular dish detergent, and hot water, your air fryer will come back to life, even with the toughest of buildup.

We've experimented with various makes and models and had our fair share of epic disasters in our air fryers, but guess what? After letting the basket and/or tray cool, we were easily able to get the buildup off with a regular kitchen sponge and hot soapy water.

Plus, even when switching between seafood and a decadent dessert, the air fryer doesn't require a deep clean.

Wipe down the outside of your fryer after each use. A hot, soapy towel is all that's necessary. This helps get off any grease or food particles that may have latched on during cooking.

Your Ninja Max XL air fryer manual may say that the parts to wash are dishwasher safe, but we recommend that you hand wash them instead. Why? Because hand washing will keep your air fryer in better shape than putting it through the wear and tear of the dishwasher. Just spend 5 minutes to give it a thorough hand wash after each use, and you'll have a properly working air fryer for years to come.

BREAD AND BREAKFAST

Peppered Maple Bacon Knots

Servings: 6

Cooking Time: 8 Minutes

Ingredients:

- 1 pound maple smoked center-cut bacon
- ¼ cup maple syrup
- ¼ cup brown sugar
- coarsely cracked black peppercorns

Directions:

1. Tie each bacon strip in a loose knot and place them on a baking sheet.
2. Combine the maple syrup and brown sugar in a bowl. Brush each knot generously with this mixture and sprinkle with coarsely cracked black pepper.
3. Preheat the air fryer to 390°F.
4. Air-fry the bacon knots in batches. Place one layer of knots in the air fryer basket and air-fry for 5 minutes. Turn the bacon knots over and air-fry for an additional 3 minutes.
5. Serve warm.

Oat Bran Muffins

Servings: 8

Cooking Time: 12 Minutes

Ingredients:

- ⅔ cup oat bran
- ½ cup flour
- ¼ cup brown sugar
- 1 teaspoon baking powder
- ½ teaspoon baking soda
- ⅛ teaspoon salt
- ½ cup buttermilk
- 1 egg
- 2 tablespoons canola oil
- ½ cup chopped dates, raisins, or dried cranberries
- 24 paper muffin cups
- cooking spray

Directions:

1. Preheat air fryer to 330°F.
2. In a large bowl, combine the oat bran, flour, brown sugar, baking powder, baking soda, and salt.
3. In a small bowl, beat together the buttermilk, egg, and oil.
4. Pour buttermilk mixture into bowl with dry ingredients and stir just until moistened. Do not beat.
5. Gently stir in dried fruit.
6. Use triple baking cups to help muffins hold shape during baking. Spray them with cooking spray, place 4 sets of cups in air fryer basket at a time, and fill each one ¾ full of batter.
7. Cook for 12minutes, until top springs back when lightly touched and toothpick inserted in center comes out clean.
8. Repeat for remaining muffins.

Country Gravy

Servings: 2

Cooking Time: 7 Minutes

Ingredients:

- ¼ pound pork sausage, casings removed
- 1 tablespoon butter
- 2 tablespoons flour
- 2 cups whole milk
- ½ teaspoon salt
- freshly ground black pepper
- 1 teaspoon fresh thyme leaves

Directions:

1. Preheat a saucepan over medium heat. Add and brown the sausage, crumbling it into small pieces as it cooks. Add the butter and flour, stirring well to combine. Continue to cook for 2 minutes, stirring constantly.
2. Slowly pour in the milk, whisking as you do, and bring the mixture to a boil to thicken. Season with salt and freshly ground black pepper, lower the heat and simmer until the sauce has thickened to your desired consistency – about 5 minutes. Stir in the fresh thyme, season to taste and serve hot.

Hush Puffins

Servings: 20

Cooking Time: 8 Minutes

Ingredients:

- 1 cup buttermilk
- ¼ cup butter, melted
- 2 eggs
- 1½ cups all-purpose flour
- 1½ cups cornmeal
- ⅓ cup sugar
- 1 teaspoon baking soda
- 1 teaspoon salt
- 4 scallions, minced
- vegetable oil

Directions:

1. Combine the buttermilk, butter and eggs in a large mixing bowl. In a second bowl combine the flour, cornmeal, sugar, baking soda and salt. Add the dry ingredients to the wet ingredients, stirring just to combine. Stir in the minced scallions and refrigerate the batter for 30 minutes.
2. Shape the batter into 2-inch balls. Brush or spray the balls with oil.
3. Preheat the air fryer to 360°F.
4. Air-fry the hush puffins in two batches at 360°F for 8 minutes, turning them over after 6 minutes of the cooking process.
5. Serve warm with butter.

Pepperoni Pizza Bread

Servings: 4

Cooking Time: 15 Minutes

Ingredients:

- 7-inch round bread boule
- 2 cups grated mozzarella cheese
- 1 tablespoon dried oregano
- 1 cup pizza sauce
- 1 cup mini pepperoni or pepperoni slices, cut in quarters
- Pizza sauce for dipping (optional)

Directions:

1. Make 7 to 8 deep slices across the bread boule, leaving 1 inch of bread uncut at the bottom of every slice before you reach the cutting board. The slices should go about three quarters of the way through the boule and be about 2 inches apart from each other. Turn the bread boule 90 degrees and make 7 to 8 similar slices perpendicular to the first slices to form squares in the bread. Again, make sure you don't cut all the way through the bread.
2. Combine the mozzarella cheese and oregano in a small bowl.
3. Fill the slices in the bread with pizza sauce by gently spreading the bread apart and spooning the sauce in between the squares of bread. Top the sauce with the mozzarella cheese mixture and then the pepperoni. Do your very best to get the cheese and pepperoni in between the slices, rather than on top of the bread. Keep spreading the bread apart and stuffing the ingredients in, but be careful not to tear the bottom of the bread.
4. Preheat the air fryer to 320°F.
5. Transfer the bread boule to the air fryer basket and air-fry for 15 minutes, making sure the top doesn't get too dark. (It will just be the cheese on top that gets dark, so if you've done a good job of tucking the cheese in between the slices, this shouldn't be an issue.)
6. Carefully remove the bread from the basket with a spatula. Transfer it to a serving platter with more sauce to dip into if desired. Serve with a lot of napkins so that people can just pull the bread apart with their hands and enjoy!

Tuscan Toast

Servings: 4

Cooking Time: 5 Minutes

Ingredients:

- ¼ cup butter
- ½ teaspoon lemon juice
- ½ clove garlic
- ½ teaspoon dried parsley flakes
- 4 slices Italian bread, 1-inch thick

Directions:

1. Place butter, lemon juice, garlic, and parsley in a food processor. Process about 1 minute, or until garlic is pulverized and ingredients are well blended.
2. Spread garlic butter on both sides of bread slices.
3. Place bread slices upright in air fryer basket. (They can lie flat but cook better standing on end.)
4. Cook at 390°F for 5minutes or until toasty brown.

Apple-cinnamon-walnut Muffins

Servings: 8

Cooking Time: 11 Minutes

Ingredients:

- 1 cup flour
- ⅓ cup sugar
- 1 teaspoon baking powder
- ¼ teaspoon baking soda
- ¼ teaspoon salt
- 1 teaspoon cinnamon
- ¼ teaspoon ginger
- ¼ teaspoon nutmeg
- 1 egg
- 2 tablespoons pancake syrup, plus 2 teaspoons
- 2 tablespoons melted butter, plus 2 teaspoons
- ¾ cup unsweetened applesauce
- ½ teaspoon vanilla extract
- ¼ cup chopped walnuts
- ¼ cup diced apple
- 8 foil muffin cups, liners removed and sprayed with cooking spray

Directions:

1. Preheat air fryer to 330°F.
2. In a large bowl, stir together flour, sugar, baking powder, baking soda, salt, cinnamon, ginger, and nutmeg.
3. In a small bowl, beat egg until frothy. Add syrup, butter, applesauce, and vanilla and mix well.
4. Pour egg mixture into dry ingredients and stir just until moistened.
5. Gently stir in nuts and diced apple.
6. Divide batter among the 8 muffin cups.
7. Place 4 muffin cups in air fryer basket and cook at 330°F for 11minutes.
8. Repeat with remaining 4 muffins or until toothpick inserted in center comes out clean.

Egg And Sausage Crescent Rolls

Servings: 8

Cooking Time: 11 Minutes

Ingredients:

- 5 large eggs
- ¼ teaspoon black pepper
- ¼ teaspoon salt
- 1 tablespoon milk
- ¼ cup shredded cheddar cheese
- One 8-ounce package refrigerated crescent rolls
- 4 tablespoon pesto sauce
- 8 fully cooked breakfast sausage links, defrosted

Directions:

1. Preheat the air fryer to 320°F.
2. In a medium bowl, crack the eggs and whisk with the pepper, salt, and milk. Pour into a frying pan over medium heat and scramble. Just before the eggs are done, turn off the heat and add in the cheese. Continue to cook until the cheese has melted and the eggs are finished (about 5 minutes total). Remove from the heat.
3. Remove the crescent rolls from the package and press them flat onto a clean surface lightly dusted with flour. Add 1½ teaspoons of pesto sauce across the center of each roll. Place equal portions of eggs across all 8 rolls. Then top each roll with a sausage link and roll the dough up tight so it resembles the crescent-roll shape.
4. Lightly spray your air fryer basket with olive oil mist and place the rolls on top. Bake for 6 minutes or until the tops of the rolls are lightly browned.
5. Remove and let cool 3 to 5 minutes before serving.

Seasoned Herbed Sourdough Croutons

Servings: 4

Cooking Time: 7 Minutes

Ingredients:

- 4 cups cubed sourdough bread, 1-inch cubes (about 8 ounces)
- 1 tablespoon olive oil
- 1 teaspoon fresh thyme leaves
- ¼ – ½ teaspoon salt
- freshly ground black pepper

Directions:

1. Combine all ingredients in a bowl and taste to make sure it is seasoned to your liking.
2. Preheat the air fryer to 400°F.
3. Toss the bread cubes into the air fryer and air-fry for 7 minutes, shaking the basket once or twice while they cook.
4. Serve warm or store in an airtight container.

Garlic Parmesan Bread Ring

Servings: 6
Cooking Time: 30 Minutes

Ingredients:

- ½ cup unsalted butter, melted
- ¼ teaspoon salt (omit if using salted butter)
- ¾ cup grated Parmesan cheese
- 3 to 4 cloves garlic, minced
- 1 tablespoon chopped fresh parsley
- 1 pound frozen bread dough, defrosted
- olive oil
- 1 egg, beaten

Directions:

1. Combine the melted butter, salt, Parmesan cheese, garlic and chopped parsley in a small bowl.
2. Roll the dough out into a rectangle that measures 8 inches by 17 inches. Spread the butter mixture over the dough, leaving a half-inch border un-buttered along one of the long edges. Roll the dough from one long edge to the other, ending with the un-buttered border. Pinch the seam shut tightly. Shape the log into a circle sealing the ends together by pushing one end into the other and stretching the dough around it.
3. Cut out a circle of aluminum foil that is the same size as the air fryer basket. Brush the foil circle with oil and place an oven safe ramekin or glass in the center. Transfer the dough ring to the aluminum foil circle, around the ramekin. This will help you make sure the dough will fit in the basket and maintain its ring shape. Use kitchen shears to cut 8 slits around the outer edge of the dough ring halfway to the center. Brush the dough ring with egg wash.
4. Preheat the air fryer to 400°F for 4 minutes. When it has Preheated, brush the sides of the basket with oil and transfer the dough ring, foil circle and ramekin into the basket. Slide the drawer back into the air fryer, but do not turn the air fryer on. Let the dough rise inside the warm air fryer for 30 minutes.
5. After the bread has proofed in the air fryer for 30 minutes, set the temperature to 340°F and air-fry the bread ring for 15 minutes. Flip the bread over by inverting it onto a plate or cutting board and sliding it back into the air fryer basket. Air-fry for another 15 minutes. Let the bread cool for a few minutes before slicing the bread ring in between the slits and serving warm.

POULTRY RECIPES

Sesame Orange Chicken

Servings: 2

Cooking Time: 9 Minutes

Ingredients:

- 1 pound boneless, skinless chicken breasts, cut into cubes
- salt and freshly ground black pepper
- ¼ cup cornstarch
- 2 eggs, beaten
- 1½ cups panko breadcrumbs
- vegetable or peanut oil, in a spray bottle
- 12 ounces orange marmalade
- 1 tablespoon soy sauce
- 1 teaspoon minced ginger
- 2 tablespoons hoisin sauce
- 1 tablespoon sesame oil
- sesame seeds, toasted

Directions:

1. Season the chicken pieces with salt and pepper. Set up a dredging station. Put the cornstarch in a zipper-sealable plastic bag. Place the beaten eggs in a bowl and put the panko breadcrumbs in a shallow dish. Transfer the seasoned chicken to the bag with the cornstarch and shake well to completely coat the chicken on all sides. Remove the chicken from the bag, shaking off any excess cornstarch and dip the pieces into the egg. Let any excess egg drip from the chicken and transfer into the breadcrumbs, pressing the crumbs onto the chicken pieces with your hands. Spray the chicken pieces with vegetable or peanut oil.
2. Preheat the air fryer to 400°F.
3. Combine the orange marmalade, soy sauce, ginger, hoisin sauce and sesame oil in a saucepan. Bring the mixture to a boil on the stovetop, lower the heat and simmer for 10 minutes, until the sauce has thickened. Set aside and keep warm.
4. Transfer the coated chicken to the air fryer basket and air-fry at 400°F for 9 minutes, shaking the basket a few times during the cooking process to help the chicken cook evenly.
5. Right before serving, toss the browned chicken pieces with the sesame orange sauce. Serve over white rice with steamed broccoli. Sprinkle the sesame seeds on top.

Chicken Rochambeau

Servings: 4

Cooking Time: 20 Minutes

Ingredients:

- 1 tablespoon butter
- 4 chicken tenders, cut in half crosswise
- salt and pepper
- ¼ cup flour
- oil for misting
- 4 slices ham, ¼- to ⅜-inches thick and large enough to cover an English muffin
- 2 English muffins, split
- Sauce
- 2 tablespoons butter
- ½ cup chopped green onions
- ½ cup chopped mushrooms
- 2 tablespoons flour
- 1 cup chicken broth
- ¼ teaspoon garlic powder
- 1½ teaspoons Worcestershire sauce

Directions:

1. Place 1 tablespoon of butter in air fryer baking pan and cook at 390°F for 2minutes to melt.
2. Sprinkle chicken tenders with salt and pepper to taste, then roll in the ¼ cup of flour.
3. Place chicken in baking pan, turning pieces to coat with melted butter.
4. Cook at 390°F for 5minutes. Turn chicken pieces over, and spray tops lightly with olive oil. Cook 5minutes longer or until juices run clear. The chicken will not brown.
5. While chicken is cooking, make the sauce: In a medium saucepan, melt the 2 tablespoons of butter.
6. Add onions and mushrooms and sauté until tender, about 3minutes.
7. Stir in the flour. Gradually add broth, stirring constantly until you have a smooth gravy.
8. Add garlic powder and Worcestershire sauce and simmer on low heat until sauce thickens, about 5minutes.
9. When chicken is cooked, remove baking pan from air fryer and set aside.
10. Place ham slices directly into air fryer basket and cook at 390°F for 5minutes or until hot and beginning to sizzle a little. Remove and set aside on top of the chicken for now.
11. Place the English muffin halves in air fryer basket and cook at 390°F for 1 minute.
12. Open air fryer and place a ham slice on top of each English muffin half. Stack 2 pieces of chicken on top of each ham slice. Cook at 390°F for 1 to 2minutes to heat through.
13. Place each English muffin stack on a serving plate and top with plenty of sauce.

Crispy Fried Onion Chicken Breasts

Servings: 2

Cooking Time: 13 Minutes

Ingredients:

- ¼ cup all-purpose flour*
- salt and freshly ground black pepper
- 1 egg
- 2 tablespoons Dijon mustard
- 1½ cups crispy fried onions (like French's®)
- ½ teaspoon paprika
- 2 (5-ounce) boneless, skinless chicken breasts
- vegetable or olive oil, in a spray bottle

Directions:

1. Preheat the air fryer to 380°F.
2. Set up a dredging station with three shallow dishes. Place the flour in the first shallow dish and season well with salt and freshly ground black pepper. Combine the egg and Dijon mustard in a second shallow dish and whisk until smooth. Place the fried onions in a sealed bag and using a rolling pin, crush them into coarse crumbs. Combine these crumbs with the paprika in the third shallow dish.
3. Dredge the chicken breasts in the flour. Shake off any excess flour and dip them into the egg mixture. Let any excess egg drip off. Then coat both sides of the chicken breasts with the crispy onions. Press the crumbs onto the chicken breasts with your hands to make sure they are well adhered.
4. Spray or brush the bottom of the air fryer basket with oil. Transfer the chicken breasts to the air fryer basket and air-fry at 380°F for 13 minutes, turning the chicken over halfway through the cooking time.
5. Serve immediately.

Poblano Bake

Servings: 4

Cooking Time: 11 Minutes Per Batch

Ingredients:

- 2 large poblano peppers (approx. 5½ inches long excluding stem)
- ¾ pound ground turkey, raw
- ¾ cup cooked brown rice
- 1 teaspoon chile powder
- ½ teaspoon ground cumin
- ½ teaspoon garlic powder
- 4 ounces sharp Cheddar cheese, grated
- 1 8-ounce jar salsa, warmed

Directions:

1. Slice each pepper in half lengthwise so that you have four wide, flat pepper halves.
2. Remove seeds and membrane and discard. Rinse inside and out.
3. In a large bowl, combine turkey, rice, chile powder, cumin, and garlic powder. Mix well.
4. Divide turkey filling into 4 portions and stuff one into each of the 4 pepper halves. Press lightly to pack down.
5. Place 2 pepper halves in air fryer basket and cook at 390°F for 10minutes or until turkey is well done.
6. Top each pepper half with ¼ of the grated cheese. Cook 1 more minute or just until cheese melts.
7. Repeat steps 5 and 6 to cook remaining pepper halves.
8. To serve, place each pepper half on a plate and top with ¼ cup warm salsa.

Tandoori Chicken Legs

Servings: 2

Cooking Time: 30 Minutes

Ingredients:

- 1 cup plain yogurt
- 2 cloves garlic, minced
- 1 tablespoon grated fresh ginger
- 2 teaspoons paprika
- 2 teaspoons ground coriander
- 1 teaspoon ground turmeric
- 1 teaspoon salt
- ¼ teaspoon ground cayenne pepper
- juice of 1 lime
- 2 bone-in, skin-on chicken legs
- fresh cilantro leaves

Directions:

1. Make the marinade by combining the yogurt, garlic, ginger, spices and lime juice. Make slashes into the chicken legs to help the marinade penetrate the meat. Pour the marinade over the chicken legs, cover and let the chicken marinate for at least an hour or overnight in the refrigerator.
2. Preheat the air fryer to 380°F.
3. Transfer the chicken legs from the marinade to the air fryer basket, reserving any extra marinade. Air-fry for 15 minutes. Flip the chicken over and pour the remaining marinade over the top. Air-fry for another 15 minutes, watching to make sure it doesn't brown too much. If it does start to get too brown, you can loosely tent the chicken with aluminum foil, tucking the ends of the foil under the chicken to stop it from blowing around.
4. Serve over rice with some fresh cilantro on top.

Taquitos

Servings: 12

Cooking Time: 6 Minutes Per Batch

Ingredients:

- 1 teaspoon butter
- 2 tablespoons chopped green onions
- 1 cup cooked chicken, shredded
- 2 tablespoons chopped green chiles
- 2 ounces Pepper Jack cheese, shredded
- 4 tablespoons salsa
- ½ teaspoon lime juice
- ¼ teaspoon cumin
- ½ teaspoon chile powder
- ⅛ teaspoon garlic powder
- 12 corn tortillas
- oil for misting or cooking spray

Directions:

1. Melt butter in a saucepan over medium heat. Add green onions and sauté a minute or two, until tender.
2. Remove from heat and stir in the chicken, green chiles, cheese, salsa, lime juice, and seasonings.
3. Preheat air fryer to 390°F.
4. To soften refrigerated tortillas, wrap in damp paper towels and microwave for 30 to 60 seconds, until slightly warmed.
5. Remove one tortilla at a time, keeping others covered with the damp paper towels. Place a heaping tablespoon of filling into tortilla, roll up and secure with toothpick. Spray all sides with oil or cooking spray.
6. Place taquitos in air fryer basket, either in a single layer or stacked. To stack, leave plenty of space between taquitos and alternate the direction of the layers, 4 on the bottom lengthwise, then 4 more on top crosswise.
7. Cook for 6minutes or until brown and crispy.
8. Repeat steps 6 and 7 to cook remaining taquitos.
9. Serve hot with guacamole, sour cream, salsa or all three!

Chicken Nuggets

Servings: 20

Cooking Time: 14 Minutes Per Batch

Ingredients:

- 1 pound boneless, skinless chicken thighs, cut into 1-inch chunks
- ¾ teaspoon salt
- ½ teaspoon black pepper
- ½ teaspoon garlic powder
- ½ teaspoon onion powder
- ½ cup flour
- 2 eggs, beaten
- ½ cup panko breadcrumbs
- 3 tablespoons plain breadcrumbs
- oil for misting or cooking spray

Directions:

1. In the bowl of a food processor, combine chicken, ½ teaspoon salt, pepper, garlic powder, and onion powder. Process in short pulses until chicken is very finely chopped and well blended.
2. Place flour in one shallow dish and beaten eggs in another. In a third dish or plastic bag, mix together the panko crumbs, plain breadcrumbs, and ¼ teaspoon salt.
3. Shape chicken mixture into small nuggets. Dip nuggets in flour, then eggs, then panko crumb mixture.
4. Spray nuggets on both sides with oil or cooking spray and place in air fryer basket in a single layer, close but not overlapping.
5. Cook at 360°F for 10minutes. Spray with oil and cook 4 minutes, until chicken is done and coating is golden brown.
6. Repeat step 5 to cook remaining nuggets.

Mediterranean Stuffed Chicken Breasts

Servings: 4

Cooking Time: 24 Minutes

Ingredients:

- 4 boneless, skinless chicken breasts
- ½ teaspoon salt
- ½ teaspoon black pepper
- ½ teaspoon garlic powder
- ½ teaspoon paprika
- ½ cup canned artichoke hearts, chopped
- 4 ounces cream cheese
- ¼ cup grated Parmesan cheese

Directions:

1. Pat the chicken breasts with a paper towel. Using a sharp knife, cut a pouch in the side of each chicken breast for filling.
2. In a small bowl, mix the salt, pepper, garlic powder, and paprika. Season the chicken breasts with this mixture.
3. In a medium bowl, mix together the artichokes, cream cheese, and grated Parmesan cheese. Divide the filling between the 4 breasts, stuffing it inside the pouches. Use toothpicks to close the pouches and secure the filling.
4. Preheat the air fryer to 360°F.
5. Spray the air fryer basket liberally with cooking spray, add the stuffed chicken breasts to the basket, and spray liberally with cooking spray again. Cook for 14 minutes, carefully turn over the chicken breasts, and cook another 10 minutes. Check the temperature at 20 minutes cooking. Chicken breasts are fully cooked when the center measures 165°F. Cook in batches, if needed.

Tortilla Crusted Chicken Breast

Servings: 2

Cooking Time: 12 Minutes

Ingredients:

- ⅓ cup flour
- 1 teaspoon salt
- 1½ teaspoons chili powder
- 1 teaspoon ground cumin
- freshly ground black pepper
- 1 egg, beaten
- ¾ cup coarsely crushed yellow corn tortilla chips
- 2 (3- to 4-ounce) boneless chicken breasts
- vegetable oil
- ½ cup salsa
- ½ cup crumbled queso fresco
- fresh cilantro leaves
- sour cream or guacamole (optional)

Directions:

1. Set up a dredging station with three shallow dishes. Combine the flour, salt, chili powder, cumin and black pepper in the first shallow dish. Beat the egg in the second shallow dish. Place the crushed tortilla chips in the third shallow dish.
2. Dredge the chicken in the spiced flour, covering all sides of the breast. Then dip the chicken into the egg, coating the chicken completely. Finally, place the chicken into the tortilla chips and press the chips onto the chicken to make sure they adhere to all sides of the breast. Spray the coated chicken breasts on both sides with vegetable oil.
3. Preheat the air fryer to 380°F.
4. Air-fry the chicken for 6 minutes. Then turn the chicken breasts over and air-fry for another 6 minutes. (Increase the cooking time if you are using chicken breasts larger than 3 to 4 ounces.)
5. When the chicken has finished cooking, serve each breast with a little salsa, the crumbled queso fresco and cilantro as the finishing touch. Serve some sour cream and/or guacamole at the table, if desired.

Turkey-hummus Wraps

Servings: 4

Cooking Time: 7 Minutes Per Batch

Ingredients:

- 4 large whole wheat wraps
- ½ cup hummus
- 16 thin slices deli turkey
- 8 slices provolone cheese
- 1 cup fresh baby spinach (or more to taste)

Directions:

1. To assemble, place 2 tablespoons of hummus on each wrap and spread to within about a half inch from edges. Top with 4 slices of turkey and 2 slices of provolone. Finish with ¼ cup of baby spinach—or pile on as much as you like.
2. Roll up each wrap. You don't need to fold or seal the ends.
3. Place 2 wraps in air fryer basket, seam side down.
4. Cook at 360°F for 4minutes to warm filling and melt cheese. If you like, you can continue cooking for 3 more minutes, until the wrap is slightly crispy.
5. Repeat step 4 to cook remaining wraps.

Parmesan Chicken Fingers

Servings: 2

Cooking Time: 19 Minutes

Ingredients:

- ½ cup flour
- 1 teaspoon salt
- freshly ground black pepper
- 2 eggs, beaten
- ¾ cup seasoned panko breadcrumbs
- ¾ cup grated Parmesan cheese
- 8 chicken tenders (about 1 pound)
- OR
- 2 to 3 boneless, skinless chicken breasts, cut into strips
- vegetable oil
- marinara sauce

Directions:

1. Set up a dredging station. Combine the flour, salt and pepper in a shallow dish. Place the beaten eggs in second shallow dish, and combine the panko breadcrumbs and Parmesan cheese in a third shallow dish.
2. Dredge the chicken tenders in the flour mixture. Then dip them into the egg, and finally place the chicken in the breadcrumb mixture. Press the coating onto both sides of the chicken tenders. Place the coated chicken tenders on a baking sheet until they are all coated. Spray both sides of the chicken fingers with vegetable oil.
3. Preheat the air fryer to 360°F.
4. Air-fry the chicken fingers in two batches. Transfer half the chicken fingers to the air fryer basket and air-fry for 9 minutes, turning the chicken over halfway through the cooking time. When the second batch of chicken fingers has finished cooking, return the first batch to the air fryer with the second batch and air-fry for one minute to heat everything through.
5. Serve immediately with marinara sauce, honey-mustard, ketchup or your favorite dipping sauce.

Quick Chicken For Filling

Servings: 2

Cooking Time: 8 Minutes

Ingredients:

- 1 pound chicken tenders, skinless and boneless
- ½ teaspoon ground cumin
- ½ teaspoon garlic powder
- cooking spray

Directions:

1. Sprinkle raw chicken tenders with seasonings.
2. Spray air fryer basket lightly with cooking spray to prevent sticking.
3. Place chicken in air fryer basket in single layer.
4. Cook at 390°F for 4minutes, turn chicken strips over, and cook for an additional 4minutes.
5. Test for doneness. Thick tenders may require an additional minute or two.

APPETIZERS AND SNACKS

Dill Fried Pickles With Light Ranch Dip

Servings: 4

Cooking Time: 8 Minutes

Ingredients:

- 4 to 6 large dill pickles, sliced in half or quartered lengthwise
- ½ cup all-purpose flour*
- 2 eggs, lightly beaten
- 1 cup plain breadcrumbs*
- 1 teaspoon salt
- ⅛ teaspoon cayenne pepper
- 2 tablespoons fresh dill leaves, dried well
- vegetable oil, in a spray bottle
- Light Ranch Dip
- ¼ cup reduced-fat mayonnaise
- ¼ cup buttermilk
- ¼ cup non-fat Greek yogurt
- 1 tablespoon chopped fresh chives
- 1 tablespoon chopped fresh parsley
- 1 tablespoon lemon juice
- salt and freshly ground black pepper

Directions:

1. Dry the dill pickle spears very well with a clean kitchen towel.
2. Set up a dredging station using three shallow dishes. Place the flour in the first shallow dish. Place the eggs into the second dish. Combine the breadcrumbs, salt, cayenne and fresh dill in a food processor and process until everything is combined and the crumbs are very fine. Place the crumb mixture in the third dish.
3. Preheat the air fryer to 400°F.
4. Coat the pickles by dredging them first in the flour, then the egg, and then the breadcrumbs, pressing the crumbs on gently with your hands. Set the coated pickles on a tray and spray them on all sides with vegetable oil.
5. Air-fry one layer of pickles at a time at 400°F for 8 minutes, turning them over halfway through the cooking process and spraying lightly again if necessary. The crumbs should be nicely browned on all sides.
6. While the pickles are air-frying, make the light ranch dip by mixing everything together in a bowl. Serve the pickles warm with the dip on the side.

Potato Chips With Sour Cream And Onion Dip

Servings: 2

Cooking Time: 20 Minutes

Ingredients:

- 2 large potatoes (Yukon Gold or russet)
- vegetable or olive oil in a spray bottle
- sea salt and freshly ground black pepper
- Sour Cream and Onion Dip:
- ½ cup sour cream
- 1 tablespoon olive oil
- 2 scallions, white part only minced
- ¼ teaspoon salt
- freshly ground black pepper
- a squeeze of lemon juice (about ¼ teaspoon)

Directions:

1. Wash the potatoes well, but leave the skins on. Slice them into ⅛-inch thin slices, using a mandolin or food processor. Rinse the potatoes under cold water until the water runs clear and then let them soak in a bowl of cold water for at least 10 minutes. Drain and dry the potato slices really well in a single layer on a clean kitchen towel.
2. Preheat the air fryer to 300°F. Spray the potato chips with the oil so that both sides are evenly coated, or rub the slices between your hands with some oil if you don't have a spray bottle.
3. Air-fry in two batches at 300°F for 20 minutes, shaking the basket a few times during the cooking process so the chips crisp and brown more evenly. Season the finished chips with sea salt and freshly ground black pepper while they are still hot.
4. While the chips are air-frying, make the sour cream and onion dip by mixing together the sour cream, olive oil, scallions, salt, pepper and lemon juice. Serve the chips warm or at room temperature along with the dip.

Rumaki

Servings: 24

Cooking Time: 12 Minutes

Ingredients:

- 10 ounces raw chicken livers
- 1 can sliced water chestnuts, drained
- ¼ cup low-sodium teriyaki sauce
- 12 slices turkey bacon
- toothpicks

Directions:

1. Cut livers into 1½-inch pieces, trimming out tough veins as you slice.
2. Place livers, water chestnuts, and teriyaki sauce in small container with lid. If needed, add another tablespoon of teriyaki sauce to make sure livers are covered. Refrigerate for 1 hour.
3. When ready to cook, cut bacon slices in half crosswise.
4. Wrap 1 piece of liver and 1 slice of water chestnut in each bacon strip. Secure with toothpick.
5. When you have wrapped half of the livers, place them in the air fryer basket in a single layer.
6. Cook at 390°F for 12 minutes, until liver is done and bacon is crispy.
7. While first batch cooks, wrap the remaining livers. Repeat step 6 to cook your second batch.

Muffuletta Sliders

Servings: 8

Cooking Time: 7 Minutes

Ingredients:

- ¼ pound thin-sliced deli ham
- ¼ pound thin-sliced pastrami
- 4 ounces low-fat mozzarella cheese, grated or sliced thin
- 8 slider buns
- olive oil for misting
- 1 tablespoon sesame seeds
- Olive Mix
- ¼ cup sliced black olives
- ½ cup sliced green olives with pimentos
- ¼ cup chopped kalamata olives
- 1 teaspoon red wine vinegar
- ¼ teaspoon basil
- ⅛ teaspoon garlic powder

Directions:

1. In a small bowl, stir together all the Olive Mix ingredients.
2. Divide the meats and cheese into 8 equal portions. To assemble sliders, stack in this order: bottom bun, ham, pastrami, 2 tablespoons olive mix, cheese, top bun.
3. Mist tops of sliders lightly with oil. Sprinkle with sesame seeds.
4. Cooking 4 at a time, place sliders in air fryer basket and cook at 360°F for 7 minutes to melt cheese and heat through.

Fried Peaches

Servings: 4

Cooking Time: 8 Minutes

Ingredients:

- 2 egg whites
- 1 tablespoon water
- ¼ cup sliced almonds
- 2 tablespoons brown sugar
- ½ teaspoon almond extract
- 1 cup crisp rice cereal
- 2 medium, very firm peaches, peeled and pitted
- ¼ cup cornstarch
- oil for misting or cooking spray

Directions:

1. Preheat air fryer to 390°F.
2. Beat together egg whites and water in a shallow dish.
3. In a food processor, combine the almonds, brown sugar, and almond extract. Process until ingredients combine well and the nuts are finely chopped.
4. Add cereal and pulse just until cereal crushes. Pour crumb mixture into a shallow dish or onto a plate.
5. Cut each peach into eighths and place in a plastic bag or container with lid. Add cornstarch, seal, and shake to coat.
6. Remove peach slices from bag or container, tapping them hard to shake off the excess cornstarch. Dip in egg wash and roll in crumbs. Spray with oil.
7. Place in air fryer basket and cook for 5minutes. Shake basket, separate any that have stuck together, and spritz a little oil on any spots that aren't browning.
8. Cook for 3 minutes longer, until golden brown and crispy.

Indian Cauliflower Tikka Bites

Servings: 6

Cooking Time: 20 Minutes

Ingredients:

- 1 cup plain Greek yogurt
- 1 teaspoon fresh ginger
- 1 teaspoon minced garlic
- 1 teaspoon vindaloo
- ½ teaspoon cardamom
- ½ teaspoon paprika
- ½ teaspoon turmeric powder
- ½ teaspoon cumin powder
- 1 large head of cauliflower, washed and cut into medium-size florets
- ½ cup panko breadcrumbs
- 1 lemon, quartered

Directions:

1. Preheat the air fryer to 350°F.
2. In a large bowl, mix the yogurt, ginger, garlic, vindaloo, cardamom, paprika, turmeric, and cumin. Add the cauliflower florets to the bowl, and coat them with the yogurt.
3. Remove the cauliflower florets from the bowl and place them on a baking sheet. Sprinkle the panko breadcrumbs over the top. Place the cauliflower bites into the air fryer basket, leaving space between the florets. Depending on the size of your air fryer, you may need to make more than one batch.
4. Cook the cauliflower for 10 minutes, shake the basket, and continue cooking another 10 minutes (or until the florets are lightly browned).
5. Remove from the air fryer and keep warm. Continue to cook until all the florets are done.
6. Before serving, lightly squeeze lemon over the top. Serve warm.

Fiery Bacon-wrapped Dates

Servings: 16

Cooking Time: 6 Minutes

Ingredients:

- 8 Thin-cut bacon strips, halved widthwise (gluten-free, if a concern)
- 16 Medium or large Medjool dates, pitted
- 3 tablespoons (about ¾ ounce) Shredded semi-firm mozzarella
- 32 Pickled jalapeño rings

Directions:

1. Preheat the air fryer to 400°F.
2. Lay a bacon strip half on a clean, dry work surface. Split one date lengthwise without cutting through it, so that it opens like a pocket. Set it on one end of the bacon strip and open it a bit. Place 1 teaspoon of the shredded cheese and 2 pickled jalapeño rings in the date, then gently squeeze it together without fully closing it (just to hold the stuffing inside). Roll up the date in the bacon strip and set it bacon seam side down on a cutting board. Repeat this process with the remaining bacon strip halves, dates, cheese, and jalapeño rings.
3. Place the bacon-wrapped dates bacon seam side down in the basket. Air-fry undisturbed for 6 minutes, or until crisp and brown.
4. Use kitchen tongs to gently transfer the wrapped dates to a wire rack or serving platter. Cool for a few minutes before serving.

Potato Chips

Servings: 2

Cooking Time: 15 Minutes

Ingredients:

- 2 medium potatoes
- 2 teaspoons extra-light olive oil
- oil for misting or cooking spray
- salt and pepper

Directions:

1. Peel the potatoes.
2. Using a mandoline or paring knife, shave potatoes into thin slices, dropping them into a bowl of water as you cut them.
3. Dry potatoes as thoroughly as possible with paper towels or a clean dish towel. Toss potato slices with the oil to coat completely.
4. Spray air fryer basket with cooking spray and add potato slices.
5. Stir and separate with a fork.
6. Cook 390°F for 5minutes. Stir and separate potato slices. Cook 5 more minutes. Stir and separate potatoes again. Cook another 5minutes.
7. Season to taste.

Cherry Chipotle Bbq Chicken Wings

Servings: 2

Cooking Time: 12 Minutes

Ingredients:

- 1 teaspoon smoked paprika
- ½ teaspoon dry mustard powder
- 1 teaspoon dried oregano
- 1 teaspoon dried thyme
- ½ teaspoon chili powder
- 1 teaspoon salt
- 2 pounds chicken wings
- vegetable oil or spray
- salt and freshly ground black pepper
- 1 to 2 tablespoons chopped chipotle peppers in adobo sauce
- ⅓ cup cherry preserves ¼ cup tomato ketchup

Directions:

1. Combine the first six ingredients in a large bowl. Prepare the chicken wings by cutting off the wing tips and discarding (or freezing for chicken stock). Divide the drumettes from the win-gettes by cutting through the joint. Place the chicken wing pieces in the bowl with the spice mix. Toss or shake well to coat.
2. Preheat the air fryer to 400°F.
3. Spray the wings lightly with the vegetable oil and air-fry the wings in two batches for 10 minutes per batch, shaking the basket halfway through the cooking process. When both batches are done, toss all the wings back into the basket for another 2 minutes to heat through and finish cooking.
4. While the wings are air-frying, combine the chopped chipotle peppers, cherry preserves and ketchup in a bowl.
5. Remove the wings from the air fryer, toss them in the cherry chipotle BBQ sauce and serve with napkins!

Asian Five-spice Wings

Servings: 4

Cooking Time: 15 Minutes

Ingredients:

- 2 pounds chicken wings
- ½ cup Asian-style salad dressing
- 2 tablespoons Chinese five-spice powder

Directions:

1. Cut off wing tips and discard or freeze for stock. Cut remaining wing pieces in two at the joint.
2. Place wing pieces in a large sealable plastic bag. Pour in the Asian dressing, seal bag, and massage the marinade into the wings until well coated. Refrigerate for at least an hour.
3. Remove wings from bag, drain off excess marinade, and place wings in air fryer basket.
4. Cook at 360°F for 15minutes or until juices run clear. About halfway through cooking time, shake the basket or stir wings for more even cooking.
5. Transfer cooked wings to plate in a single layer. Sprinkle half of the Chinese five-spice powder on the wings, turn, and sprinkle other side with remaining seasoning.

Avocado Toast With Lemony Shrimp

Servings: 4

Cooking Time: 6 Minutes

Ingredients:

- 6 ounces Raw medium shrimp (30 to 35 per pound), peeled and deveined
- 1½ teaspoons Finely grated lemon zest
- 2 teaspoons Lemon juice
- 1½ teaspoons Minced garlic
- 1½ teaspoons Ground black pepper
- 4 Rye or whole-wheat bread slices (gluten-free, if a concern)
- 2 Ripe Hass avocado(s), halved, pitted, peeled and roughly chopped
- For garnishing Coarse sea salt or kosher salt

Directions:

1. Preheat the air fryer to 400°F.
2. Toss the shrimp, lemon zest, lemon juice, garlic, and pepper in a bowl until the shrimp are evenly coated.
3. When the machine is at temperature, use kitchen tongs to place the shrimp in a single layer in the basket. Air-fry undisturbed for 4 minutes, or until the shrimp are pink and barely firm. Use kitchen tongs to transfer the shrimp to a cutting board.
4. Working in batches, set as many slices of bread as will fit in the basket in one layer. Air-fry undisturbed for 2 minutes, just until warmed through and crisp. The bread will not brown much.
5. Arrange the bread slices on a clean, dry work surface. Divide the avocado bits among them and gently smash the avocado into a coarse paste with the tines of a flatware fork. Top the toasts with the shrimp and sprinkle with salt as a garnish.

Sausage And Cheese Rolls

Servings: 3

Cooking Time: 18 Minutes

Ingredients:

- 3 3- to 3½-ounce sweet or hot Italian sausage links
- 2 1-ounce string cheese stick(s), unwrapped and cut in half lengthwise
- Three quarters from one thawed sheet (cut the sheet into four quarters; wrap and refreeze one of them) A 17.25-ounce box frozen puff pastry

Directions:

1. Preheat the air fryer to 400°F.
2. When the machine is at temperature, set the sausage links in the basket and air-fry undisturbed for 12 minutes, or until cooked through.
3. Use kitchen tongs to transfer the links to a wire rack. Cool for 15 minutes. (If necessary, pour out any rendered fat that has collected below the basket in the machine.)
4. Cut the sausage links in half lengthwise. Sandwich half a string cheese stick between two sausage halves, trimming the ends so the cheese doesn't stick out beyond the meat.
5. Roll each piece of puff pastry into a 6 x 6-inch square on a clean, dry work surface. Set the sausage-cheese sandwich at one edge and roll it up in the dough. The ends will be open like a pig-in-a-blanket. Repeat with the remaining puff pastry, sausage, and cheese.
6. Set the rolls seam side down in the basket. Air-fry undisturbed for 6 minutes, or until puffed and golden brown.
7. Use a nonstick-safe spatula, and perhaps a flatware fork for balance, to transfer the rolls to a wire rack. Cool for at least 5 minutes before serving.

VEGETABLE SIDE DISHES RECIPES

Roasted Garlic

Servings: 20

Cooking Time: 40 Minutes

Ingredients:

- 20 Peeled medium garlic cloves
- 2 tablespoons, plus more Olive oil

Directions:

1. Preheat the air fryer to 400°F.
2. Set a 10-inch sheet of aluminum foil on your work surface for a small batch, a 14-inch sheet for a medium batch, or a 16-inch sheet for a large batch. Put the garlic cloves in its center in one layer without bunching the cloves together. (Spread them out a little for even cooking.) Drizzle the small batch with 1 tablespoon oil, the medium batch with 2 tablespoons, or the large one with 3 tablespoons. Fold up the sides and seal the foil into a packet.
3. When the machine is at temperature, put the packet in the basket. Air-fry for 40 minutes, or until very fragrant. The cloves inside should be golden and soft.
4. Transfer the packet to a cutting board. Cool for 5 minutes, then open and use the cloves hot. Or cool them to room temperature, set them in a small container or jar, pour in enough olive oil to cover them, seal or cover the container, and refrigerate for up to 2 weeks.

Spicy Fried Green Beans

Servings: 2

Cooking Time: 8 Minutes

Ingredients:

- 12 ounces green beans, trimmed
- 2 small dried hot red chili peppers (like árbol)
- ¼ cup panko breadcrumbs
- 1 tablespoon olive oil
- ½ teaspoon salt
- ⅛ teaspoon crushed red pepper flakes
- 2 scallions, thinly sliced

Directions:

1. Preheat the air fryer to 400°F.
2. Toss the green beans, chili peppers and panko breadcrumbs with the olive oil, salt and crushed red pepper flakes.
3. Air-fry for 8 minutes (depending on the size of the beans), shaking the basket once during the cooking process. The crumbs will fall into the bottom drawer – don't worry.
4. Transfer the green beans to a serving dish, sprinkle the scallions and the toasted crumbs from the air fryer drawer on top and serve. The dried peppers are not to be eaten, but they do look nice with the green beans. You can leave them in, or take them out as you please.

Chicken Eggrolls

Servings: 10

Cooking Time: 17 Minutes

Ingredients:

- 1 tablespoon vegetable oil
- ¼ cup chopped onion
- 1 clove garlic, minced
- 1 cup shredded carrot
- ½ cup thinly sliced celery
- 2 cups cooked chicken
- 2 cups shredded white cabbage
- ½ cup teriyaki sauce
- 20 egg roll wrappers
- 1 egg, whisked
- 1 tablespoon water

Directions:

1. Preheat the air fryer to 390°F.
2. In a large skillet, heat the oil over medium-high heat. Add in the onion and sauté for 1 minute. Add in the garlic and sauté for 30 seconds. Add in the carrot and celery and cook for 2 minutes. Add in the chicken, cabbage, and teriyaki sauce. Allow the mixture to cook for 1 minute, stirring to combine. Remove from the heat.
3. In a small bowl, whisk together the egg and water for brushing the edges.
4. Lay the eggroll wrappers out at an angle. Place ¼ cup filling in the center. Fold the bottom corner up first and then fold in the corners; roll up to complete eggroll.
5. Place the eggrolls in the air fryer basket, spray with cooking spray, and cook for 8 minutes, turn over, and cook another 2 to 4 minutes.

Parmesan Asparagus

Servings: 2

Cooking Time: 5 Minutes

Ingredients:

- 1 bunch asparagus, stems trimmed
- 1 teaspoon olive oil
- salt and freshly ground black pepper
- ¼ cup coarsely grated Parmesan cheese
- ½ lemon

Directions:

1. Preheat the air fryer to 400°F.
2. Toss the asparagus with the oil and season with salt and freshly ground black pepper.
3. Transfer the asparagus to the air fryer basket and air-fry at 400°F for 5 minutes, shaking the basket to turn the asparagus once or twice during the cooking process.
4. When the asparagus is cooked to your liking, sprinkle the asparagus generously with the Parmesan cheese and close the air fryer drawer again. Let the asparagus sit for 1 minute in the turned-off air fryer. Then, remove the asparagus, transfer it to a serving dish and finish with a grind of black pepper and a squeeze of lemon juice.

Onions

Servings: 4

Cooking Time: 18 Minutes

Ingredients:

- 2 yellow onions (Vidalia or 1015 recommended)
- salt and pepper
- ¼ teaspoon ground thyme
- ¼ teaspoon smoked paprika
- 2 teaspoons olive oil
- 1 ounce Gruyère cheese, grated

Directions:

1. Peel onions and halve lengthwise (vertically).
2. Sprinkle cut sides of onions with salt, pepper, thyme, and paprika.
3. Place each onion half, cut-surface up, on a large square of aluminum foil. Pull sides of foil up to cup around onion. Drizzle cut surface of onions with oil.
4. Crimp foil at top to seal closed.
5. Place wrapped onions in air fryer basket and cook at 390°F for 18 minutes. When done, onions should be soft enough to pierce with fork but still slightly firm.
6. Open foil just enough to sprinkle each onion with grated cheese.
7. Cook for 30 seconds to 1 minute to melt cheese.

Charred Radicchio Salad

Servings: 4

Cooking Time: 5 Minutes

Ingredients:

- 2 Small 5- to 6-ounce radicchio head(s)
- 3 tablespoons Olive oil
- ½ teaspoon Table salt
- 2 tablespoons Balsamic vinegar
- Up to ¼ teaspoon Red pepper flakes

Directions:

1. Preheat the air fryer to 375°F .
2. Cut the radicchio head(s) into quarters through the stem end. Brush the oil over the heads, particularly getting it between the leaves along the cut sides. Sprinkle the radicchio quarters with the salt.
3. When the machine is at temperature, set the quarters cut sides up in the basket with as much air space between them as possible. They should not touch. Air-fry undisturbed for 5 minutes, watching carefully because they burn quickly, until blackened in bits and soft.
4. Use a nonstick-safe spatula to transfer the quarters to a cutting board. Cool for a minute or two, then cut out the thick stems inside the heads. Discard these tough bits and chop the remaining heads into bite-size bits. Scrape them into a bowl. Add the vinegar and red pepper flakes. Toss well and serve warm.

General Tso's Cauliflower

Servings: 3

Cooking Time: 15 Minutes

Ingredients:

- ⅓ cup All-purpose flour or tapioca flour
- 2 Large egg(s), well beaten
- ⅔ cup Plain panko bread crumbs (gluten-free, if a concern)
- 2½ cups (about 13 ounces) 1½-inch cauliflower florets
- Vegetable oil spray
- 2 tablespoons Regular or low-sodium soy sauce or gluten-free tamari sauce
- 1 tablespoon Hoisin sauce (gluten-free, if a concern; see here)
- 1 tablespoon Unseasoned rice vinegar (see here)
- 2 teaspoons Granulated white sugar
- 1½ teaspoons Sriracha or other hot red pepper sauce (gluten-free, if a concern)
- Not needed Water
- Not needed Cornstarch

Directions:

1. Preheat the air fryer to 400°F.
2. Put the flour in one zip-closed plastic bag, the beaten egg in a second bag, and the bread crumbs in a third.
3. Put the cauliflower florets in the bag with the flour. Seal closed, then shake and turn to coat the florets completely. Open the bag and transfer the florets to the bag with the egg(s). (Do not just dump the florets from one bag into the other.) Seal the second bag and turn gently to coat the florets in the egg(s). Open the second bag and use kitchen tongs to transfer the florets to the third bag. Seal that bag; shake and turn it to coat the florets in the bread crumbs.
4. Spread paper towels on your work surface. Gently transfer the florets to these paper towels, then coat them with vegetable oil spray on all sides.
5. Gently spread the florets in the basket in as close to one layer as you can. Air-fry undisturbed for 15 minutes, or until crisp and browned.
6. Meanwhile, stir the soy sauce or tamari sauce, hoisin sauce, vinegar, sugar, and sriracha in a small saucepan set over medium heat until smooth. Bring to a simmer, stirring often. Because of the small amount of liquid, the small and medium batches will not need to be thickened. Simply remove the saucepan from the heat.
7. For the large batch, whisk the water and cornstarch in a small bowl until smooth, then whisk this slurry into the soy or tamari mixture in the saucepan. Cook about 1 minute, whisking constantly, until thickened. Remove from the heat.
8. When the cauliflower florets are done, dump them into a large bowl. Pour the mixture in the saucepan over them. Toss well to coat. Serve warm.

Cheesy Potato Pot

Servings: 4

Cooking Time: 13 Minutes

Ingredients:

- 3 cups cubed red potatoes (unpeeled, cut into ½-inch cubes)
- ½ teaspoon garlic powder
- salt and pepper
- 1 tablespoon oil
- chopped chives for garnish (optional)
- Sauce
- 2 tablespoons milk
- 1 tablespoon butter
- 2 ounces sharp Cheddar cheese, grated
- 1 tablespoon sour cream

Directions:

1. Place potato cubes in large bowl and sprinkle with garlic, salt, and pepper. Add oil and stir to coat well.
2. Cook at 390°F for 13 minutes or until potatoes are tender. Stir every 4 or 5minutes during cooking time.
3. While potatoes are cooking, combine milk and butter in a small saucepan. Warm over medium-low heat to melt butter. Add cheese and stir until it melts. The melted cheese will remain separated from the milk mixture. Remove from heat until potatoes are done.
4. When ready to serve, add sour cream to cheese mixture and stir over medium-low heat just until warmed. Place cooked potatoes in serving bowl. Pour sauce over potatoes and stir to combine.
5. Garnish with chives if desired.

Fried Eggplant Slices

Servings: 3

Cooking Time: 12 Minutes

Ingredients:

- 1½ sleeves (about 60 saltines) Saltine crackers
- ¾ cup Cornstarch
- 2 Large egg(s), well beaten
- 1 medium (about ¾ pound) Eggplant, stemmed, peeled, and cut into ¼-inch-thick rounds
- Olive oil spray

Directions:

1. Preheat the air fryer to 400°F. Also, position the rack in the center of the oven and heat the oven to 175°F.
2. Grind the saltines, in batches if necessary, in a food processor, pulsing the machine and rearranging the saltine pieces every few pulses. Or pulverize the saltines in a large, heavy zip-closed plastic bag with the bottom of a heavy saucepan. In either case, you want small bits of saltines, not just crumbs.
3. Set up and fill three shallow soup plates or small pie plates on your counter: one for the cornstarch, one for the beaten egg(s), and one for the pulverized saltines.
4. Set an eggplant slice in the cornstarch and turn it to coat on both sides. Use a brush to lightly remove any excess. Dip it into the beaten egg(s) and turn to coat both sides. Let any excess egg slip back into the rest, then set the slice in the saltines. Turn several times, pressing gently to coat both sides evenly but not heavily. Coat both sides of the slice with olive oil spray and set it aside. Continue dipping and coating the remaining slices.
5. Set one, two, or maybe three slices in the basket. There should be at least ½ inch between them for proper air flow. Air-fry undisturbed for 12 minutes, or until crisp and browned.
6. Use a nonstick-safe spatula to transfer the slice(s) to a large baking sheet. Slip it into the oven to keep the slices warm as you air-fry more batches, as needed, always transferring the slices to the baking sheet to stay warm.

Five-spice Roasted Sweet Potatoes

Servings: 4

Cooking Time: 12 Minutes

Ingredients:

- ½ teaspoon ground cinnamon
- ¼ teaspoon ground cumin
- ¼ teaspoon paprika
- 1 teaspoon chile powder
- ⅛ teaspoon turmeric
- ½ teaspoon salt (optional)
- freshly ground black pepper
- 2 large sweet potatoes, peeled and cut into ¾-inch cubes (about 3 cups)
- 1 tablespoon olive oil

Directions:

1. In a large bowl, mix together cinnamon, cumin, paprika, chile powder, turmeric, salt, and pepper to taste.
2. Add potatoes and stir well.
3. Drizzle the seasoned potatoes with the olive oil and stir until evenly coated.
4. Place seasoned potatoes in the air fryer baking pan or an ovenproof dish that fits inside your air fryer basket.
5. Cook for 6minutes at 390°F, stop, and stir well.
6. Cook for an additional 6minutes.

Steakhouse Baked Potatoes

Servings: 3

Cooking Time: 55 Minutes

Ingredients:

- 3 10-ounce russet potatoes
- 2 tablespoons Olive oil
- 1 teaspoon Table salt

Directions:

1. Preheat the air fryer to 375°F .
2. Poke holes all over each potato with a fork. Rub the skin of each potato with 2 teaspoons of the olive oil, then sprinkle ¼ teaspoon salt all over each potato.
3. When the machine is at temperature, set the potatoes in the basket in one layer with as much air space between them as possible. Air-fry for 50 minutes, turning once, or until soft to the touch but with crunchy skins. If the machine is at 360°F, you may need to add up to 5 minutes to the cooking time.
4. Use kitchen tongs to gently transfer the baked potatoes to a wire rack. Cool for 5 or 10 minutes before serving.

Mushrooms, Sautéed

Servings: 4

Cooking Time: 4 Minutes

Ingredients:

- 8 ounces sliced white mushrooms, rinsed and well drained
- ¼ teaspoon garlic powder
- 1 tablespoon Worcestershire sauce

Directions:

1. Place mushrooms in a large bowl and sprinkle with garlic powder and Worcestershire. Stir well to distribute seasonings evenly.
2. Place in air fryer basket and cook at 390°F for 4 minutes, until tender.

BEEF， PORK & LAMB RECIPES

Steak Fingers

Servings: 4

Cooking Time: 8 Minutes

Ingredients:

- 4 small beef cube steaks
- salt and pepper
- ½ cup flour
- oil for misting or cooking spray

Directions:

1. Cut cube steaks into 1-inch-wide strips.
2. Sprinkle lightly with salt and pepper to taste.
3. Roll in flour to coat all sides.
4. Spray air fryer basket with cooking spray or oil.
5. Place steak strips in air fryer basket in single layer, very close together but not touching. Spray top of steak strips with oil or cooking spray.
6. Cook at 390°F for 4minutes, turn strips over, and spray with oil or cooking spray.
7. Cook 4 more minutes and test with fork for doneness. Steak fingers should be crispy outside with no red juices inside. If needed, cook an additional 4 minutes or until well done. (Don't eat beef cube steak rare.)
8. Repeat steps 5 through 7 to cook remaining strips.

Steakhouse Burgers With Red Onion Compote

Servings: 4

Cooking Time: 22 Minutes

Ingredients:

- 1½ pounds lean ground beef
- 2 cloves garlic, minced and divided
- 1 teaspoon Worcestershire sauce
- 1 teaspoon sea salt, divided
- ½ teaspoon black pepper
- 1 tablespoon extra-virgin olive oil
- 1 red onion, thinly sliced
- ¼ cup balsamic vinegar
- 1 teaspoon sugar
- 1 tablespoon tomato paste
- 2 tablespoons mayonnaise
- 2 tablespoons sour cream
- 4 brioche hamburger buns
- 1 cup arugula

Directions:

1. In a large bowl, mix together the ground beef, 1 of the minced garlic cloves, the Worcestershire sauce, ½ teaspoon of the salt, and the black pepper. Form the meat into 1-inch-thick patties. Make a dent in the center (this helps the center cook evenly). Let the meat sit for 15 minutes.
2. Meanwhile, in a small saucepan over medium heat, cook the olive oil and red onion for 4 minutes, stirring frequently to avoid burning. Add in the balsamic vinegar, sugar, and tomato paste, and cook for an additional 3 minutes, stirring frequently. Transfer the onion compote to a small bowl.
3. Preheat the air fryer to 350°F.
4. In another small bowl, mix together the remaining minced garlic, the mayonnaise, and the sour cream. Spread the mayo mixture on the insides of the brioche buns.
5. Cook the hamburgers for 6 minutes, flip the burgers, and cook an additional 2 to 6 minutes. Check the internal temperature to avoid under- or overcooking. Hamburgers should be cooked to at least 160°F. After cooking, cover with foil and let the meat rest for 5 minutes.
6. Meanwhile, place the buns inside the air fryer and toast them for 3 minutes.
7. To assemble the burgers, place the hamburger on one side of the bun, top with onion compote and ¼ cup arugula, and then place the other half of the bun on top.

Garlic And Oregano Lamb Chops

Servings: 4

Cooking Time: 17 Minutes

Ingredients:

- 1½ tablespoons Olive oil
- 1 tablespoon Minced garlic
- 1 teaspoon Dried oregano
- 1 teaspoon Finely minced orange zest
- ¾ teaspoon Fennel seeds
- ¾ teaspoon Table salt
- ¾ teaspoon Ground black pepper
- 6 4-ounce, 1-inch-thick lamb loin chops

Directions:

1. Mix the olive oil, garlic, oregano, orange zest, fennel seeds, salt, and pepper in a large bowl. Add the chops and toss well to coat. Set aside as the air fryer heats, tossing one more time.
2. Preheat the air fryer to 400°F.
3. Set the chops bone side down in the basket (that is, so they stand up on their bony edge) with as much air space between them as possible. Air-fry undisturbed for 14 minutes for medium-rare, or until an instant-read meat thermometer inserted into the thickest part of a chop (without touching bone) registers 132°F (not USDA-approved). Or air-fry undisturbed for 17 minutes for well done, or until an instant-read meat thermometer registers 145°F (USDA-approved).
4. Use kitchen tongs to transfer the chops to a wire rack. Cool for 5 minutes before serving.

Tuscan Veal Chops

Servings: 2

Cooking Time: 12-15 Minutes

Ingredients:

- 4 teaspoons Olive oil
- 2 teaspoons Finely minced garlic
- 2 teaspoons Finely minced fresh rosemary leaves
- 1 teaspoon Finely grated lemon zest
- 1 teaspoon Crushed fennel seeds
- 1 teaspoon Table salt
- Up to ¼ teaspoon Red pepper flakes
- 2 10-ounce bone-in veal loin or rib chop(s), about ½ inch thick

Directions:

1. Preheat the air fryer to 400°F.
2. Mix the oil, garlic, rosemary, lemon zest, fennel seeds, salt, and red pepper flakes in a small bowl. Rub this mixture onto both sides of the veal chop(s). Set aside at room temperature as the machine comes to temperature.
3. Set the chop(s) in the basket. If you're cooking more than one chop, leave as much air space between them as possible. Air-fry undisturbed for 12 minutes for medium-rare, or until an instant-read meat thermometer inserted into the center of a chop (without touching bone) registers 135°F (not USDA-approved). Or air-fry undisturbed for 15 minutes for medium-well, or until an instant-read meat thermometer registers 145°F (USDA-approved).
4. Use kitchen tongs to transfer the chops to a cutting board or a wire rack. Cool for 5 minutes before serving.

Better-than-chinese-take-out Pork Ribs

Servings: 3

Cooking Time: 35 Minutes

Ingredients:

- 1½ tablespoons Hoisin sauce (see here; gluten-free, if a concern)
- 1½ tablespoons Regular or low-sodium soy sauce or gluten-free tamari sauce
- 1½ tablespoons Shaoxing (Chinese cooking rice wine), dry sherry, or white grape juice
- 1½ teaspoons Minced garlic
- ¾ teaspoon Ground dried ginger
- ¾ teaspoon Ground white pepper
- 1½ pounds Pork baby back rib rack(s), cut into 2-bone pieces

Directions:

1. Mix the hoisin sauce, soy or tamari sauce, Shaoxing or its substitute, garlic, ginger, and white pepper in a large bowl. Add the rib sections and stir well to coat. Cover and refrigerate for at least 2 hours or up to 24 hours, stirring the rib sections in the marinade occasionally.
2. Preheat the air fryer to 350°F . Set the ribs in their bowl on the counter as the machine heats.
3. When the machine is at temperature, set the rib pieces on their sides in a single layer in the basket with as much air space between them as possible. Air-fry for 35 minutes, turning and rearranging the pieces once, until deeply browned and sizzling.
4. Use kitchen tongs to transfer the rib pieces to a large serving bowl or platter. Wait a minute or two before serving them so the meat can reabsorb some of its own juices.

Mongolian Beef

Servings: 4

Cooking Time: 15 Minutes

Ingredients:

- 1½ pounds flank steak, thinly sliced
- on the bias into ¼-inch strips
- Marinade
- 2 tablespoons soy sauce*
- 1 clove garlic, smashed
- big pinch crushed red pepper flakes
- Sauce
- 1 tablespoon vegetable oil
- 2 cloves garlic, minced
- 1 tablespoon finely grated fresh ginger
- 3 dried red chili peppers
- ¾ cup soy sauce*
- ¾ cup chicken stock
- 5 to 6 tablespoons brown sugar (depending on how sweet you want the sauce)
- ½ cup cornstarch, divided
- 1 bunch scallions, sliced into 2-inch pieces

Directions:

1. Marinate the beef in the soy sauce, garlic and red pepper flakes for one hour.
2. In the meantime, make the sauce. Preheat a small saucepan over medium heat on the stovetop. Add the oil, garlic, ginger and dried chili peppers and sauté for just a minute or two. Add the soy sauce, chicken stock and brown sugar and continue to simmer for a few minutes. Dissolve 3 tablespoons of cornstarch in 3 tablespoons of water and stir this into the saucepan. Stir the sauce over medium heat until it thickens. Set this aside.
3. Preheat the air fryer to 400°F.
4. Remove the beef from the marinade and transfer it to a zipper sealable plastic bag with the remaining cornstarch. Shake it around to completely coat the beef and transfer the coated strips of beef to a baking sheet or plate, shaking off any excess cornstarch. Spray the strips with vegetable oil on all sides and transfer them to the air fryer basket.
5. Air-fry at 400°F for 15 minutes, shaking the basket to toss and rotate the beef strips throughout the cooking process. Add the scallions for the last 4 minutes of the cooking. Transfer the hot beef strips and scallions to a bowl and toss with the sauce (warmed on the stovetop if necessary), coating all the beef strips with the sauce. Serve warm over white rice.

Korean-style Lamb Shoulder Chops

Servings: 3

Cooking Time: 28 Minutes

Ingredients:

- ⅓ cup Regular or low-sodium soy sauce or gluten-free tamari sauce
- 1½ tablespoons Toasted sesame oil
- 1½ tablespoons Granulated white sugar
- 2 teaspoons Minced peeled fresh ginger
- 1 teaspoon Minced garlic
- ¼ teaspoon Red pepper flakes
- 3 6-ounce bone-in lamb shoulder chops, any excess fat trimmed
- ⅔ cup Tapioca flour
- Vegetable oil spray

Directions:

1. Put the soy or tamari sauce, sesame oil, sugar, ginger, garlic, and red pepper flakes in a large, heavy zip-closed plastic bag. Add the chops, seal, and rub the marinade evenly over them through the bag. Refrigerate for at least 2 hours or up to 6 hours, turning the bag at least once so the chops move around in the marinade.
2. Set the bag out on the counter as the air fryer heats. Preheat the air fryer to 375°F .
3. Pour the tapioca flour on a dinner plate or in a small pie plate. Remove a chop from the marinade and dredge it on both sides in the tapioca flour, coating it evenly and well. Coat both sides with vegetable oil spray, set it in the basket, and dredge and spray the remaining chop(s), setting them in the basket in a single layer with space between them. Discard the bag with the marinade.
4. Air-fry, turning once, for 25 minutes, or until the chops are well browned and tender when pierced with the point of a paring knife. If the machine is at 360°F, you may need to add up to 3 minutes to the cooking time.
5. Use kitchen tongs to transfer the chops to a wire rack. Cool for just a couple of minutes before serving.

Sweet And Sour Pork

Servings: 2

Cooking Time: 11 Minutes

Ingredients:

- ⅓ cup all-purpose flour
- ⅓ cup cornstarch
- 2 teaspoons Chinese 5-spice powder
- 1 teaspoon salt
- freshly ground black pepper
- 1 egg
- 2 tablespoons milk
- ¾ pound boneless pork, cut into 1-inch cubes
- vegetable or canola oil, in a spray bottle
- 1½ cups large chunks of red and green peppers
- ½ cup ketchup
- 2 tablespoons rice wine vinegar or apple cider vinegar
- 2 tablespoons brown sugar
- ¼ cup orange juice
- 1 tablespoon soy sauce
- 1 clove garlic, minced
- 1 cup cubed pineapple
- chopped scallions

Directions:

1. Set up a dredging station with two bowls. Combine the flour, cornstarch, Chinese 5-spice powder, salt and pepper in one large bowl. Whisk the egg and milk together in a second bowl. Dredge the pork cubes in the flour mixture first, then dip them into the egg and then back into the flour to coat on all sides. Spray the coated pork cubes with vegetable or canola oil.
2. Preheat the air fryer to 400°F.
3. Toss the pepper chunks with a little oil and air-fry at 400°F for 5 minutes, shaking the basket halfway through the cooking time.
4. While the peppers are cooking, start making the sauce. Combine the ketchup, rice wine vinegar, brown sugar, orange juice, soy sauce, and garlic in a medium saucepan and bring the mixture to a boil on the stovetop. Reduce the heat and simmer for 5 minutes. When the peppers have finished air-frying, add them to the saucepan along with the pineapple chunks. Simmer the peppers and pineapple in the sauce for an additional 2 minutes. Set aside and keep warm.
5. Add the dredged pork cubes to the air fryer basket and air-fry at 400°F for 6 minutes, shaking the basket to turn the cubes over for the last minute of the cooking process.
6. When ready to serve, toss the cooked pork with the pineapple, peppers and sauce. Serve over white rice and garnish with chopped scallions.

Crispy Lamb Shoulder Chops

Servings: 3

Cooking Time: 28 Minutes

Ingredients:

- ¾ cup All-purpose flour or gluten-free all-purpose flour
- 2 teaspoons Mild paprika
- 2 teaspoons Table salt
- 1½ teaspoons Garlic powder
- 1½ teaspoons Dried sage leaves
- 3 6-ounce bone-in lamb shoulder chops, any excess fat trimmed
- Olive oil spray

Directions:

1. Whisk the flour, paprika, salt, garlic powder, and sage in a large bowl until the mixture is of a uniform color. Add the chops and toss well to coat. Transfer them to a cutting board.
2. Preheat the air fryer to 375°F .
3. When the machine is at temperature, again dredge the chops one by one in the flour mixture. Lightly coat both sides of each chop with olive oil spray before putting it in the basket. Continue on with the remaining chop(s), leaving air space between them in the basket.
4. Air-fry, turning once, for 25 minutes, or until the chops are well browned and tender when pierced with the point of a paring knife. If the machine is at 360°F, you may need to add up to 3 minutes to the cooking time.
5. Use kitchen tongs to transfer the chops to a wire rack. Cool for 5 minutes before serving.

Tuscan Chimichangas

Servings: 2

Cooking Time: 8 Minutes

Ingredients:

- ¼ pound Thinly sliced deli ham, chopped
- 1 cup Drained and rinsed canned white beans
- ½ cup (about 2 ounces) Shredded semi-firm mozzarella
- ¼ cup Chopped sun-dried tomatoes
- ¼ cup Bottled Italian salad dressing, vinaigrette type
- 2 Burrito-size (12-inch) flour tortilla(s)
- Olive oil spray

Directions:

1. Preheat the air fryer to 375°F .
2. Mix the ham, beans, cheese, tomatoes, and salad dressing in a bowl.
3. Lay a tortilla on a clean, dry work surface. Put all of the ham mixture in a narrow oval in the middle of the tortilla, if making one burrito; or half of this mixture, if making two. Fold the parts of the tortilla that are closest to the ends of the filling oval up and over the filling, then roll the tortilla tightly closed, but don't press down hard. Generously coat the tortilla with olive oil spray. Make a second filled tortilla, if necessary.
4. Set the filled tortilla(s) seam side down in the basket, with at least ½ inch between them, if making two. Air-fry undisturbed for 8 minutes, or until crisp and lightly browned.
5. Use kitchen tongs and a nonstick-safe spatula to transfer the chimichanga(s) to a wire rack. Cool for 5 minutes before serving.

Bacon Wrapped Filets Mignons

Servings: 4

Cooking Time: 18 Minutes

Ingredients:

- 4 slices bacon (not thick cut)
- 4 (8-ounce) filets mignons
- 1 tablespoon fresh thyme leaves
- salt and freshly ground black pepper

Directions:

1. Preheat the air fryer to 400°F.
2. Lay the bacon slices down on a cutting board and sprinkle the thyme leaves on the bacon slices. Remove any string tying the filets and place the steaks down on their sides on top of the bacon slices. Roll the bacon around the side of the filets and secure the bacon to the fillets with a toothpick or two.
3. Season the steaks generously with salt and freshly ground black pepper and transfer the steaks to the air fryer.
4. Air-fry for 18 minutes, turning the steaks over halfway through the cooking process. This should cook your steaks to about medium, depending on how thick they are. If you'd prefer your steaks medium-rare or medium-well, simply add or subtract two minutes from the cooking time. Remove the steaks from the air fryer and let them rest for 5 minutes before removing the toothpicks and serving. (Just enough time to quickly air-fry some vegetables to go with them!)

Venison Backstrap

Servings: 4

Cooking Time: 10 Minutes

Ingredients:

- 2 eggs
- ¼ cup milk
- 1 cup whole wheat flour
- ½ teaspoon salt
- ¼ teaspoon pepper
- 1 pound venison backstrap, sliced
- salt and pepper
- oil for misting or cooking spray

Directions:

1. Beat together eggs and milk in a shallow dish.
2. In another shallow dish, combine the flour, salt, and pepper. Stir to mix well.
3. Sprinkle venison steaks with additional salt and pepper to taste. Dip in flour, egg wash, then in flour again, pressing in coating.
4. Spray steaks with oil or cooking spray on both sides.
5. Cooking in 2 batches, place steaks in the air fryer basket in a single layer. Cook at 360°F for 8minutes. Spray with oil, turn over, and spray other side. Cook for 2 minutes longer, until coating is crispy brown and meat is done to your liking.
6. Repeat to cook remaining venison.

DESSERTS AND SWEETS

Mixed Berry Hand Pies

Servings: 4

Cooking Time: 15 Minutes

Ingredients:

- ¾ cup sugar
- ½ teaspoon ground cinnamon
- 1 tablespoon cornstarch
- 1 cup blueberries
- 1 cup blackberries
- 1 cup raspberries, divided
- 1 teaspoon water
- 1 package refrigerated pie dough (or your own homemade pie dough)
- 1 egg, beaten

Directions:

1. Combine the sugar, cinnamon, and cornstarch in a small saucepan. Add the blueberries, blackberries, and ½ cup of the raspberries. Toss the berries gently to coat them evenly. Add the teaspoon of water to the saucepan and turn the stovetop on to medium-high heat, stirring occasionally. Once the berries break down, release their juice and start to simmer (about 5 minutes), simmer for another couple of minutes and then transfer the mixture to a bowl, stir in the remaining ½ cup of raspberries and let it cool.
2. Preheat the air fryer to 370°F.
3. Cut the pie dough into four 5-inch circles and four 6-inch circles.
4. Spread the 6-inch circles on a flat surface. Divide the berry filling between all four circles. Brush the perimeter of the dough circles with a little water. Place the 5-inch circles on top of the filling and press the perimeter of the dough circles together to seal. Roll the edges of the bottom circle up over the top circle to make a crust around the filling. Press a fork around the crust to make decorative indentations and to seal the crust shut. Brush the pies with egg wash and sprinkle a little sugar on top. Poke a small hole in the center of each pie with a paring knife to vent the dough.
5. Air-fry two pies at a time. Brush or spray the air fryer basket with oil and place the pies into the basket. Air-fry for 9 minutes. Turn the pies over and air-fry for another 6 minutes. Serve warm or at room temperature.

Giant Buttery Chocolate Chip Cookie

Servings: 4

Cooking Time: 16 Minutes

Ingredients:

- ⅔ cup plus 1 tablespoon All-purpose flour
- ¼ teaspoon Baking soda
- ¼ teaspoon Table salt
- Baking spray (see the headnote)
- 4 tablespoons (¼ cup/½ stick) plus 1 teaspoon Butter, at room temperature
- ¼ cup plus 1 teaspoon Packed dark brown sugar
- 3 tablespoons plus 1 teaspoon Granulated white sugar
- 2½ tablespoons Pasteurized egg substitute, such as Egg Beaters
- ½ teaspoon Vanilla extract
- ¾ cup plus 1 tablespoon Semisweet or bittersweet chocolate chips

Directions:

1. Preheat the air fryer to 350°F .
2. Whisk the flour, baking soda, and salt in a bowl until well combined.
3. For a small air fryer, coat the inside of a 6-inch round cake pan with baking spray. For a medium air fryer, coat the inside of a 7-inch round cake pan with baking spray. And for a large air fryer, coat the inside of an 8-inch round cake pan with baking spray.
4. Using a hand electric mixer at medium speed, beat the butter, brown sugar, and granulated white sugar in a bowl until smooth and thick, about 3 minutes, scraping down the inside of the bowl several times.
5. Beat in the pasteurized egg substitute or egg (as applicable) and vanilla until uniform. Scrape down and remove the beaters. Fold in the flour mixture and chocolate chips with a rubber spatula, just until combined. Scrape and gently press this dough into the prepared pan, getting it even across the pan to the perimeter.
6. Set the pan in the basket and air-fry undisturbed for 16 minutes, or until the cookie is puffed, browned, and feels set to the touch.
7. Transfer the pan to a wire rack and cool for 10 minutes. Loosen the cookie from the perimeter with a spatula, then invert the pan onto a cutting board and let the cookie come free. Remove the pan and reinvert the cookie onto the wire rack. Cool for 5 minutes more before slicing into wedges to serve.

Thumbprint Sugar Cookies

Servings: 10

Cooking Time: 8 Minutes

Ingredients:

- 2½ tablespoons butter
- ⅓ cup cane sugar
- 1 teaspoon pure vanilla extract
- 1 large egg
- 1 cup all-purpose flour
- ½ teaspoon baking soda
- ¼ teaspoon salt
- 10 chocolate kisses

Directions:

1. Preheat the air fryer to 350°F.
2. In a large bowl, cream the butter with the sugar and vanilla. Whisk in the egg and set aside.
3. In a separate bowl, mix the flour, baking soda, and salt. Then gently mix the dry ingredients into the wet. Portion the dough into 10 balls; then press down on each with the bottom of a cup to create a flat cookie.
4. Liberally spray the metal trivet of an air fryer basket with olive oil mist.
5. Place the cookies in the air fryer basket on the trivet and cook for 8 minutes or until the tops begin to lightly brown.
6. Remove and immediately press the chocolate kisses into the tops of the cookies while still warm.
7. Let cool 5 minutes and then enjoy.

Giant Buttery Oatmeal Cookie

Servings: 4

Cooking Time: 16 Minutes

Ingredients:

- 1 cup Rolled oats (not quick-cooking or steel-cut oats)
- ½ cup All-purpose flour
- ½ teaspoon Baking soda
- ½ teaspoon Ground cinnamon
- ½ teaspoon Table salt
- 3½ tablespoons Butter, at room temperature
- ⅓ cup Packed dark brown sugar
- 1½ tablespoons Granulated white sugar
- 3 tablespoons (or 1 medium egg, well beaten) Pasteurized egg substitute, such as Egg Beaters
- ¾ teaspoon Vanilla extract
- ⅓ cup Chopped pecans
- Baking spray

Directions:

1. Preheat the air fryer to 350°F .
2. Stir the oats, flour, baking soda, cinnamon, and salt in a bowl until well combined.
3. Using an electric hand mixer at medium speed , beat the butter, brown sugar, and granulated white sugar until creamy and thick, about 3 minutes, scraping down the inside of the bowl occasionally. Beat in the egg substitute or egg (as applicable) and vanilla until uniform.
4. Scrape down and remove the beaters. Fold in the flour mixture and pecans with a rubber spatula just until all the flour is moistened and the nuts are even throughout the dough.
5. For a small air fryer, coat the inside of a 6-inch round cake pan with baking spray. For a medium air fryer, coat the inside of a 7-inch round cake pan with baking spray. And for a large air fryer, coat the inside of an 8-inch round cake pan with baking spray. Scrape and gently press the dough into the prepared pan, spreading it into an even layer to the perimeter.
6. Set the pan in the basket and air-fry undisturbed for 16 minutes, or until puffed and browned.
7. Transfer the pan to a wire rack and cool for 10 minutes. Loosen the cookie from the perimeter with a spatula, then invert the pan onto a cutting board and let the cookie come free. Remove the pan and reinvert the cookie onto the wire rack. Cool for 5 minutes more before slicing into wedges to serve.

Keto Cheesecake Cups

Servings: 6

Cooking Time: 10 Minutes

Ingredients:

- 8 ounces cream cheese
- ¼ cup plain whole-milk Greek yogurt
- 1 large egg
- 1 teaspoon pure vanilla extract
- 3 tablespoons monk fruit sweetener
- ¼ teaspoon salt
- ½ cup walnuts, roughly chopped

Directions:

1. Preheat the air fryer to 315°F.
2. In a large bowl, use a hand mixer to beat the cream cheese together with the yogurt, egg, vanilla, sweetener, and salt. When combined, fold in the chopped walnuts.
3. Set 6 silicone muffin liners inside an air-fryer-safe pan. Note: This is to allow for an easier time getting the cheesecake bites in and out. If you don't have a pan, you can place them directly in the air fryer basket.
4. Evenly fill the cupcake liners with cheesecake batter.
5. Carefully place the pan into the air fryer basket and cook for about 10 minutes, or until the tops are lightly browned and firm.
6. Carefully remove the pan when done and place in the refrigerator for 3 hours to firm up before serving.

Air-fried Strawberry Hand Tarts

Servings: 9

Cooking Time: 9 Minutes

Ingredients:

- ½ cup butter, softened
- ½ cup sugar
- 2 eggs
- 1 teaspoon vanilla extract
- 2 tablespoons lemon zest
- 2½ cups all-purpose flour
- 1 teaspoon baking powder
- ¼ teaspoon salt
- 1¼ cups strawberry jam, divided
- 1 egg white, beaten
- 1 cup powdered sugar
- 2 teaspoons milk

Directions:

1. Combine the butter and sugar in a bowl and beat with an electric mixer until the mixture is light and fluffy. Add the eggs one at a time. Add the vanilla extract and lemon zest and mix well. In a separate bowl, combine the flour, baking powder and salt. Add the dry ingredients to the wet ingredients, mixing just until the dough comes together. Transfer the dough to a floured surface and knead by hand for 10 minutes. Cover with a clean kitchen towel and let the dough rest for 30 minutes. (Alternatively, dough can be mixed and kneaded in a stand mixer.)
2. Divide the dough in half and roll each half out into a ¼-inch thick rectangle that measures 12-inches x 9-inches. Cut each rectangle of dough into nine 4-inch x 3-inch rectangles (a pizza cutter is very helpful for this task). You should have 18 rectangles. Spread two teaspoons of strawberry jam in the center of nine of the rectangles leaving a ¼-inch border around the edges. Brush the egg white around the edges of each rectangle and top with the remaining nine rectangles of dough. Press the back of a fork around the edges to seal the tarts shut. Brush the top of the tarts with the beaten egg white and pierce the dough three or four times down the center of the tart with a fork.
3. Preheat the air fryer to 350°F.
4. Air-fry the tarts in batches at 350°F for 6 minutes. Flip the tarts over and air-fry for an additional 3 minutes.
5. While the tarts are air-frying, make the icing. Combine the powdered sugar, ¼ cup strawberry preserves and milk in a bowl, whisking until the icing is smooth. Spread the icing over the top of each tart, leaving an empty border around the edges. Decorate with sprinkles if desired.

Cheese Blintzes

Servings: 6

Cooking Time: 10 Minutes

Ingredients:

- 1½ 7½-ounce package(s) farmer cheese
- 3 tablespoons Regular or low-fat cream cheese (not fat-free)
- 3 tablespoons Granulated white sugar
- ¼ teaspoon Vanilla extract
- 6 Egg roll wrappers
- 3 tablespoons Butter, melted and cooled

Directions:

1. Preheat the air fryer to 375°F .
2. Use a flatware fork to mash the farmer cheese, cream cheese, sugar, and vanilla in a small bowl until smooth.
3. Set one egg roll wrapper on a clean, dry work surface. Place ¼ cup of the filling at the edge closest to you, leaving a ½-inch gap before the edge of the wrapper. Dip your clean finger in water and wet the edges of the wrapper. Fold the perpendicular sides over the filling, then roll the wrapper closed with the filling inside. Set it aside seam side down and continue filling the remainder of the wrappers.
4. Brush the wrappers on all sides with the melted butter. Be generous. Set them seam side down in the basket with as much space between them as possible. Air-fry undisturbed for 10 minutes, or until lightly browned.
5. Use a nonstick-safe spatula to transfer the blintzes to a wire rack. Cool for at least 5 minutes or up to 20 minutes before serving.

Vanilla Butter Cake

Servings: 6

Cooking Time: 20-24 Minutes

Ingredients:

- ¾ cup plus 1 tablespoon All-purpose flour
- 1 teaspoon Baking powder
- ¼ teaspoon Table salt
- 8 tablespoons (½ cup/1 stick) Butter, at room temperature
- ½ cup Granulated white sugar
- 2 Large egg(s)
- 2 tablespoons Whole or low-fat milk (not fat-free)
- ¾ teaspoon Vanilla extract
- Baking spray (see here)

Directions:

1. Preheat the air fryer to 325°F (or 330°F, if that's the closest setting).
2. Mix the flour, baking powder, and salt in a small bowl until well combined.
3. Using an electric hand mixer at medium speed, beat the butter and sugar in a medium bowl until creamy and smooth, about 3 minutes, occasionally scraping down the inside of the bowl.
4. Beat in the egg or eggs, as well as the white or a yolk as necessary. Beat in the milk and vanilla until smooth. Turn off the beaters and add the flour mixture. Beat at low speed until thick and smooth.
5. Use the baking spray to generously coat the inside of a 6-inch round cake pan for a small batch, a 7-inch round cake pan for a medium batch, or an 8-inch round cake pan for a large batch. Scrape and spread the batter into the pan, smoothing the batter out to an even layer.
6. Set the pan in the basket and air-fry undisturbed for 20 minutes for a 6-inch layer, 22 minutes for a 7-inch layer, or 24 minutes for an 8-inch layer, or until a toothpick or cake tester inserted into the center of the cake comes out clean. Start checking it at the 15-minute mark to know where you are.
7. Use hot pads or silicone baking mitts to transfer the cake pan to a wire rack. Cool for 5 minutes. To unmold, set a cutting board over the baking pan and invert both the board and the pan. Lift the still-warm pan off the cake layer. Set the wire rack on top of the cake layer and invert all of it with the cutting board so that the cake layer is now right side up on the wire rack. Remove the cutting board and continue cooling the cake for at least 10 minutes or to room temperature, about 30 minutes, before slicing into wedges.

Glazed Cherry Turnovers

Servings: 8

Cooking Time: 14 Minutes

Ingredients:

- 2 sheets frozen puff pastry, thawed
- 1 (21-ounce) can premium cherry pie filling
- 2 teaspoons ground cinnamon
- 1 egg, beaten
- 1 cup sliced almonds
- 1 cup powdered sugar
- 2 tablespoons milk

Directions:

1. Roll a sheet of puff pastry out into a square that is approximately 10-inches by 10-inches. Cut this large square into quarters.
2. Mix the cherry pie filling and cinnamon together in a bowl. Spoon ¼ cup of the cherry filling into the center of each puff pastry square. Brush the perimeter of the pastry square with the egg wash. Fold one corner of the puff pastry over the cherry pie filling towards the opposite corner, forming a triangle. Seal the two edges of the pastry together with the tip of a fork, making a design with the tines. Brush the top of the turnovers with the egg wash and sprinkle sliced almonds over each one. Repeat these steps with the second sheet of puff pastry. You should have eight turnovers at the end.
3. Preheat the air fryer to 370°F.
4. Air-fry two turnovers at a time for 14 minutes, carefully turning them over halfway through the cooking time.
5. While the turnovers are cooking, make the glaze by whisking the powdered sugar and milk together in a small bowl until smooth. Let the glaze sit for a minute so the sugar can absorb the milk. If the consistency is still too thick to drizzle, add a little more milk, a drop at a time, and stir until smooth.
6. Let the cooked cherry turnovers sit for at least 10 minutes. Then drizzle the glaze over each turnover in a zigzag motion. Serve warm or at room temperature.

Orange Gooey Butter Cake

Servings: 6

Cooking Time: 85 Minutes

Ingredients:

- Crust Layer:
- ½ cup flour
- ¼ cup sugar
- ½ teaspoon baking powder
- ⅛ teaspoon salt
- 2 ounces (½ stick) unsalted European style butter, melted
- 1 egg
- 1 teaspoon orange extract
- 2 tablespoons orange zest
- Gooey Butter Layer:
- 8 ounces cream cheese, softened
- 4 ounces (1 stick) unsalted European style butter, melted
- 2 eggs
- 2 teaspoons orange extract
- 2 tablespoons orange zest
- 4 cups powdered sugar
- Garnish:
- powdered sugar
- orange slices

Directions:

1. Preheat the air fryer to 350°F.
2. Grease a 7-inch cake pan and line the bottom with parchment paper. Combine the flour, sugar, baking powder and salt in a bowl. Add the melted butter, egg, orange extract and orange zest. Mix well and press this mixture into the bottom of the greased cake pan. Lower the pan into the basket using an aluminum foil sling (fold a piece of aluminum foil into a strip about 2-inches wide by 24-inches long). Fold the ends of the aluminum foil over the top of the dish before returning the basket to the air fryer. Air-fry uncovered for 8 minutes.
3. To make the gooey butter layer, beat the cream cheese, melted butter, eggs, orange extract and orange zest in a large bowl using an electric hand mixer. Add the powdered sugar in stages, beat until smooth with each addition. Pour this mixture on top of the baked crust in the cake pan. Wrap the pan with a piece of greased aluminum foil, tenting the top of the foil to leave a little room for the cake to rise.
4. Air-fry for 60 minutes at 350°F. Remove the aluminum foil and air-fry for an additional 17 minutes.
5. Let the cake cool inside the pan for at least 10 minutes. Then, run a butter knife around the cake and let the cake cool completely in the pan. When cooled, run the butter knife around the edges of the cake again and invert it onto a plate and then back onto a serving platter. Sprinkle the powdered sugar over the top of the cake and garnish with orange slices.

Dark Chocolate Peanut Butter S'mores

Servings: 4

Cooking Time: 6 Minutes

Ingredients:

- 4 graham cracker sheets
- 4 marshmallows
- 4 teaspoons chunky peanut butter
- 4 ounces dark chocolate
- ½ teaspoon ground cinnamon

Directions:

1. Preheat the air fryer to 390°F. Break the graham crackers in half so you have 8 pieces.
2. Place 4 pieces of graham cracker on the bottom of the air fryer. Top each with one of the marshmallows and bake for 6 or 7 minutes, or until the marshmallows have a golden brown center.
3. While cooking, slather each of the remaining graham crackers with 1 teaspoon peanut butter.
4. When baking completes, carefully remove each of the graham crackers, add 1 ounce of dark chocolate on top of the marshmallow, and lightly sprinkle with cinnamon. Top with the remaining peanut butter graham cracker to make the sandwich. Serve immediately.

Roasted Vegetable Stromboli

Servings: 2

Cooking Time: 29 Minutes

Ingredients:

- ½ onion, thinly sliced
- ½ red pepper, julienned
- ½ yellow pepper, julienned
- olive oil
- 1 small zucchini, thinly sliced
- 1 cup thinly sliced mushrooms
- 1½ cups chopped broccoli
- 1 teaspoon Italian seasoning
- salt and freshly ground black pepper
- ½ recipe of Blue Jean Chef Pizza dough (page 231) OR 1 (14-ounce) tube refrigerated pizza dough
- 2 cups grated mozzarella cheese
- ¼ cup grated Parmesan cheese
- ½ cup sliced black olives, optional
- dried oregano
- pizza or marinara sauce

Directions:

1. Preheat the air fryer to 400°F.
2. Toss the onions and peppers with a little olive oil and air-fry the vegetables for 7 minutes, shaking the basket once or twice while the vegetables cook. Add the zucchini, mushrooms, broccoli and Italian seasoning to the basket. Add a little more olive oil and season with salt and freshly ground black pepper. Air-fry for an additional 7 minutes, shaking the basket halfway through. Let the vegetables cool slightly while you roll out the pizza dough.
3. On a lightly floured surface, roll or press the pizza dough out into a 13-inch by 11-inch rectangle, with the long side closest to you. Sprinkle half of the mozzarella and Parmesan cheeses over the dough leaving an empty 1-inch border from the edge farthest away from you. Spoon the roasted vegetables over the cheese, sprinkle the olives over everything and top with the remaining cheese.
4. Start rolling the stromboli away from you and toward the empty border. Make sure the filling stays tightly tucked inside the roll. Finally, tuck the ends of the dough in and pinch the seam shut. Place the seam side down and shape the stromboli into a U-shape to fit into the air fryer basket. Cut 4 small slits with the tip of a sharp knife evenly in the top of the dough, lightly brush the stromboli with a little oil and sprinkle with some dried oregano.
5. Preheat the air fryer to 360°F.
6. Spray or brush the air fryer basket with oil and transfer the U-shaped stromboli to the air fryer basket. Air-fry for 15 minutes, flipping the stromboli over after the first 10 minutes. (Use a plate to invert the Stromboli out of the air fryer basket and then slide it back into the basket off the plate.)
7. To remove, carefully flip the stromboli over onto a cutting board. Let it rest for a couple of minutes before serving. Cut it into 2-inch slices and serve with pizza or marinara sauce.

Roasted Vegetable Lasagna

Servings: 6

Cooking Time: 55 Minutes

Ingredients:

- 1 zucchini, sliced
- 1 yellow squash, sliced
- 8 ounces mushrooms, sliced
- 1 red bell pepper, cut into 2-inch strips
- 1 tablespoon olive oil
- 2 cups ricotta cheese
- 2 cups grated mozzarella cheese, divided
- 1 egg
- 1 teaspoon salt
- freshly ground black pepper
- ¼ cup shredded carrots
- ½ cup chopped fresh spinach
- 8 lasagna noodles, cooked
- Béchamel Sauce:
- 3 tablespoons butter
- 3 tablespoons flour
- 2½ cups milk
- ½ cup grated Parmesan cheese
- ½ teaspoon salt
- freshly ground black pepper
- pinch of ground nutmeg

Directions:

1. Preheat the air fryer to 400°F.
2. Toss the zucchini, yellow squash, mushrooms and red pepper in a large bowl with the olive oil and season with salt and pepper. Air-fry for 10 minutes, shaking the basket once or twice while the vegetables cook.
3. While the vegetables are cooking, make the béchamel sauce and cheese filling. Melt the butter in a medium saucepan over medium-high heat on the stovetop. Add the flour and whisk, cooking for a couple of minutes. Add the milk and whisk vigorously until smooth. Bring the mixture to a boil and simmer until the sauce thickens. Stir in the Parmesan cheese and season with the salt, pepper and nutmeg. Set the sauce aside.
4. Combine the ricotta cheese, 1¼ cups of the mozzarella cheese, egg, salt and pepper in a large bowl and stir until combined. Fold in the carrots and spinach.
5. When the vegetables have finished cooking, build the lasagna. Use a baking dish that is 6 inches in diameter and 4 inches high. Cover the bottom of the baking dish with a little béchamel sauce. Top with two lasagna noodles, cut to fit the dish and overlapping each other a little. Spoon a third of the ricotta cheese mixture and then a third of the roasted veggies on top of the noodles. Pour ½ cup of béchamel sauce on top and then repeat these layers two more times: noodles – cheese mixture – vegetables –

béchamel sauce. Sprinkle the remaining mozzarella cheese over the top. Cover the dish with aluminum foil, tenting it loosely so the aluminum doesn't touch the cheese.

6. Lower the dish into the air fryer basket using an aluminum foil sling (fold a piece of aluminum foil into a strip about 2-inches wide by 24-inches long). Fold the ends of the aluminum foil over the top of the dish before returning the basket to the air fryer. Air-fry for 45 minutes, removing the foil for the last 2 minutes, to slightly brown the cheese on top.
7. Let the lasagna rest for at least 20 minutes to set up a little before slicing into it and serving.

Stuffed Zucchini Boats

Servings: 2

Cooking Time: 20 Minutes

Ingredients:

- olive oil
- ½ cup onion, finely chopped
- 1 clove garlic, finely minced
- ½ teaspoon dried oregano
- ¼ teaspoon dried thyme
- ¾ cup couscous
- 1½ cups chicken stock, divided
- 1 tomato, seeds removed and finely chopped
- ½ cup coarsely chopped Kalamata olives
- ½ cup grated Romano cheese
- ¼ cup pine nuts, toasted
- 1 tablespoon chopped fresh parsley
- 1 teaspoon salt
- freshly ground black pepper
- 1 egg, beaten
- 1 cup grated mozzarella cheese, divided
- 2 thick zucchini

Directions:

1. Preheat a sauté pan on the stovetop over medium-high heat. Add the olive oil and sauté the onion until it just starts to soften–about 4 minutes. Stir in the garlic, dried oregano and thyme. Add the couscous and sauté for just a minute. Add 1¼ cups of the chicken stock and simmer over low heat for 3 to 5 minutes, until liquid has been absorbed and the couscous is soft. Remove the pan from heat and set it aside to cool slightly.
2. Fluff the couscous and add the tomato, Kalamata olives, Romano cheese, pine nuts, parsley, salt and pepper. Mix well. Add the remaining chicken stock, the egg and ½ cup of the mozzarella cheese. Stir to ensure everything is combined.
3. Cut each zucchini in half lengthwise. Then, trim each half of the zucchini into four 5-inch lengths. (Save the trimmed ends of the zucchini for another use.) Use a spoon to scoop out the center of the zucchini, leaving some flesh around the sides. Brush both sides of the zucchini with olive oil and season the cut side with salt and pepper.
4. Preheat the air fryer to 380°F.
5. Divide the couscous filling between the four zucchini boats. Use your hands to press the filling together and fill the inside of the zucchini. The filling should be mounded into the boats and rounded on top.
6. Transfer the zucchini boats to the air fryer basket and drizzle the stuffed zucchini boats with olive oil. Air-fry for 19 minutes. Then, sprinkle the remaining mozzarella cheese on top of the zucchini, pressing it down onto the filling lightly to prevent it from blowing around in the air fryer. Air-fry for one more minute to melt the cheese. Transfer the finished zucchini boats to a serving platter and garnish with the chopped parsley.

Mexican Twice Air-fried Sweet Potatoes

Servings: 2

Cooking Time: 42 Minutes

Ingredients:

- 2 large sweet potatoes
- olive oil
- salt and freshly ground black pepper
- ⅓ cup diced red onion
- ⅓ cup diced red bell pepper
- ½ cup canned black beans, drained and rinsed
- ½ cup corn kernels, fresh or frozen
- ½ teaspoon chili powder
- 1½ cups grated pepper jack cheese, divided
- Jalapeño peppers, sliced

Directions:

1. Preheat the air fryer to 400°F.
2. Rub the outside of the sweet potatoes with olive oil and season with salt and freshly ground black pepper. Transfer the potatoes into the air fryer basket and air-fry at 400°F for 30 minutes, rotating the potatoes a few times during the cooking process.
3. While the potatoes are air-frying, start the potato filling. Preheat a large sauté pan over medium heat on the stovetop. Add the onion and pepper and sauté for a few minutes, until the vegetables start to soften. Add the black beans, corn, and chili powder and sauté for another 3 minutes. Set the mixture aside.
4. Remove the sweet potatoes from the air fryer and let them rest for 5 minutes. Slice off one inch of the flattest side of both potatoes. Scrape the potato flesh out of the potatoes, leaving half an inch of potato flesh around the edge of the potato. Place all the potato flesh into a large bowl and mash it with a fork. Add the black bean mixture and 1 cup of the pepper jack cheese to the mashed sweet potatoes. Season with salt and freshly ground black pepper and mix well. Stuff the hollowed out potato shells with the black bean and sweet potato mixture, mounding the filling high in the potatoes.
5. Transfer the stuffed potatoes back into the air fryer basket and air-fry at 370°F for 10 minutes. Sprinkle the remaining cheese on top of each stuffed potato, lower the heat to 340°F and air-fry for an additional 2 minutes to melt the cheese. Top with a couple slices of Jalapeño pepper and serve warm with a green salad.

Pizza Portobello Mushrooms

Servings: 2

Cooking Time: 18 Minutes

Ingredients:

- 2 portobello mushroom caps, gills removed (see Figure 13-1)
- 1 teaspoon extra-virgin olive oil
- ¼ cup diced onion
- 1 teaspoon minced garlic
- 1 medium zucchini, shredded
- 1 teaspoon dried oregano
- ½ teaspoon black pepper
- ¼ teaspoon salt
- ⅓ cup marinara sauce
- ¼ cup shredded part-skim mozzarella cheese
- ¼ teaspoon red pepper flakes
- 2 tablespoons Parmesan cheese
- 2 tablespoons chopped basil

Directions:

1. Preheat the air fryer to 370°F.
2. Lightly spray the mushrooms with an olive oil mist and place into the air fryer to cook for 10 minutes, cap side up.
3. Add the olive oil to a pan and sauté the onion and garlic together for about 2 to 4 minutes. Stir in the zucchini, oregano, pepper, and salt, and continue to cook. When the zucchini has cooked down (usually about 4 to 6 minutes), add in the marinara sauce. Remove from the heat and stir in the mozzarella cheese.
4. Remove the mushrooms from the air fryer basket when cooking completes. Reset the temperature to 350°F.
5. Using a spoon, carefully stuff the mushrooms with the zucchini marinara mixture.
6. Return the stuffed mushrooms to the air fryer basket and cook for 5 to 8 minutes, or until the cheese is lightly browned. You should be able to easily insert a fork into the mushrooms when they're cooked.
7. Remove the mushrooms and sprinkle the red pepper flakes, Parmesan cheese, and fresh basil over the top.
8. Serve warm.

Broccoli Cheddar Stuffed Potatoes

Servings: 2

Cooking Time: 42 Minutes

Ingredients:

- 2 large russet potatoes, scrubbed
- 1 tablespoon olive oil
- salt and freshly ground black pepper
- 2 tablespoons butter
- ¼ cup sour cream
- 3 tablespoons half-and-half (or milk)
- 1¼ cups grated Cheddar cheese, divided
- ¾ teaspoon salt
- freshly ground black pepper
- 1 cup frozen baby broccoli florets, thawed and drained

Directions:

1. Preheat the air fryer to 400°F.
2. Rub the potatoes all over with olive oil and season generously with salt and freshly ground black pepper. Transfer the potatoes into the air fryer basket and air-fry for 30 minutes, turning the potatoes over halfway through the cooking process.
3. Remove the potatoes from the air fryer and let them rest for 5 minutes. Cut a large oval out of the top of both potatoes. Leaving half an inch of potato flesh around the edge of the potato, scoop the inside of the potato out and into a large bowl to prepare the potato filling. Mash the scooped potato filling with a fork and add the butter, sour cream, half-and-half, 1 cup of the grated Cheddar cheese, salt and pepper to taste. Mix well and then fold in the broccoli florets.
4. Stuff the hollowed out potato shells with the potato and broccoli mixture. Mound the filling high in the potatoes – you will have more filling than room in the potato shells.
5. Transfer the stuffed potatoes back to the air fryer basket and air-fry at 360°F for 10 minutes. Sprinkle the remaining Cheddar cheese on top of each stuffed potato, lower the heat to 330°F and air-fry for an additional minute or two to melt cheese.

Thai Peanut Veggie Burgers

Servings: 6

Cooking Time: 14 Minutes

Ingredients:

- One 15.5-ounce can cannellini beans
- 1 teaspoon minced garlic
- ¼ cup chopped onion
- 1 Thai chili pepper, sliced
- 2 tablespoons natural peanut butter
- ½ teaspoon black pepper
- ½ teaspoon salt
- ⅓ cup all-purpose flour (optional)
- ½ cup cooked quinoa
- 1 large carrot, grated
- 1 cup shredded red cabbage
- ¼ cup peanut dressing
- ¼ cup chopped cilantro
- 6 Hawaiian rolls
- 6 butterleaf lettuce leaves

Directions:

1. Preheat the air fryer to 350°F.
2. To a blender or food processor fitted with a metal blade, add the beans, garlic, onion, chili pepper, peanut butter, pepper, and salt. Pulse for 5 to 10 seconds. Do not over process. The mixture should be coarse, not smooth.
3. Remove from the blender or food processor and spoon into a large bowl. Mix in the cooked quinoa and carrots. At this point, the mixture should begin to hold together to form small patties. If the dough appears to be too sticky (meaning you likely processed a little too long), add the flour to hold the patties together.
4. Using a large spoon, form 8 equal patties out of the batter.
5. Liberally spray a metal trivet with olive oil spray and set in the air fryer basket. Place the patties into the basket, leaving enough space to be able to turn them with a spatula.
6. Cook for 7 minutes, flip, and cook another 7 minutes.
7. Remove from the heat and repeat with additional patties.
8. To serve, place the red cabbage in a bowl and toss with peanut dressing and cilantro. Place the veggie burger on a bun, and top with a slice of lettuce and cabbage slaw.

Cheesy Enchilada Stuffed Baked Potatoes

Servings: 4 Cooking Time: 37 Minutes

Ingredients:

- 2 medium russet potatoes, washed
- One 15-ounce can mild red enchilada sauce
- One 15-ounce can low-sodium black beans, rinsed and drained
- 1 teaspoon taco seasoning
- ½ cup shredded cheddar cheese
- 1 medium avocado, halved
- ½ teaspoon garlic powder
- ¼ teaspoon black pepper
- ¼ teaspoon salt
- 2 teaspoons fresh lime juice
- 2 tablespoon chopped red onion
- ¼ cup chopped cilantro

Directions:

1. Preheat the air fryer to 390°F.
2. Puncture the outer surface of the potatoes with a fork.
3. Set the potatoes inside the air fryer basket and cook for 20 minutes, rotate, and cook another 10 minutes.
4. In a large bowl, mix the enchilada sauce, black beans, and taco seasoning.
5. When the potatoes have finished cooking, carefully remove them from the air fryer basket and let cool for 5 minutes.
6. Using a pair of tongs to hold the potato if it's still too hot to touch, slice the potato in half lengthwise. Use a spoon to scoop out the potato flesh and add it into the bowl with the enchilada sauce. Mash the potatoes with the enchilada sauce mixture, creating a uniform stuffing.
7. Place the potato skins into an air-fryer-safe pan and stuff the halves with the enchilada stuffing. Sprinkle the cheese over the top of each potato.
8. Set the air fryer temperature to 350°F, return the pan to the air fryer basket, and cook for another 5 to 7 minutes to heat the potatoes and melt the cheese.
9. While the potatoes are cooking, take the avocado and scoop out the flesh into a small bowl. Mash it with the back of a fork; then mix in the garlic powder, pepper, salt, lime juice, and onion. Set aside.
10. When the potatoes have finished cooking, remove the pan from the air fryer and place the potato halves on a plate. Top with avocado mash and fresh cilantro. Serve immediately.

Egg Rolls

Servings: 4

Cooking Time: 8 Minutes

Ingredients:

- 1 clove garlic, minced
- 1 teaspoon sesame oil
- 1 teaspoon olive oil
- ½ cup chopped celery
- ½ cup grated carrots
- 2 green onions, chopped
- 2 ounces mushrooms, chopped
- 2 cups shredded Napa cabbage
- 1 teaspoon low-sodium soy sauce
- 1 teaspoon cornstarch
- salt
- 1 egg
- 1 tablespoon water
- 4 egg roll wraps
- olive oil for misting or cooking spray

Directions:

1. In a large skillet, sauté garlic in sesame and olive oils over medium heat for 1 minute.
2. Add celery, carrots, onions, and mushrooms to skillet. Cook 1 minute, stirring.
3. Stir in cabbage, cover, and cook for 1 minute or just until cabbage slightly wilts.
4. In a small bowl, mix soy sauce and cornstarch. Stir into vegetables to thicken. Remove from heat. Salt to taste if needed.
5. Beat together egg and water in a small bowl.
6. Divide filling into 4 portions and roll up in egg roll wraps. Brush all over with egg wash to seal.
7. Mist egg rolls very lightly with olive oil or cooking spray and place in air fryer basket.
8. Cook at 390°F for 4minutes. Turn over and cook 4 more minutes, until golden brown and crispy.

Basic Fried Tofu

Servings: 4

Cooking Time: 17 Minutes

Ingredients:

- 14 ounces extra-firm tofu, drained and pressed
- 1 tablespoon sesame oil
- 2 tablespoons low-sodium soy sauce
- ¼ cup rice vinegar
- 1 tablespoon fresh grated ginger
- 1 clove garlic, minced
- 3 tablespoons cornstarch
- ¼ teaspoon black pepper
- ⅛ teaspoon salt

Directions:

1. Cut the tofu into 16 cubes. Set aside in a glass container with a lid.
2. In a medium bowl, mix the sesame oil, soy sauce, rice vinegar, ginger, and garlic. Pour over the tofu and secure the lid. Place in the refrigerator to marinate for an hour.
3. Preheat the air fryer to 350°F.
4. In a small bowl, mix the cornstarch, black pepper, and salt.
5. Transfer the tofu to a large bowl and discard the leftover marinade. Pour the cornstarch mixture over the tofu and toss until all the pieces are coated.
6. Liberally spray the air fryer basket with olive oil mist and set the tofu pieces inside. Allow space between the tofu so it can cook evenly. Cook in batches if necessary.
7. Cook 15 to 17 minutes, shaking the basket every 5 minutes to allow the tofu to cook evenly on all sides. When it's done cooking, the tofu will be crisped and browned on all sides.
8. Remove the tofu from the air fryer basket and serve warm.

Asparagus, Mushroom And Cheese Soufflés

Servings: 3

Cooking Time: 21 Minutes

Ingredients:

- butter
- grated Parmesan cheese
- 3 button mushrooms, thinly sliced
- 8 spears asparagus, sliced ½-inch long
- 1 teaspoon olive oil
- 1 tablespoon butter
- 4½ teaspoons flour
- pinch paprika
- pinch ground nutmeg
- salt and freshly ground black pepper
- ½ cup milk
- ½ cup grated Gruyère cheese or other Swiss cheese (about 2 ounces)
- 2 eggs, separated

Directions:

1. Butter three 6-ounce ramekins and dust with grated Parmesan cheese. (Butter the ramekins and then coat the butter with Parmesan by shaking it around in the ramekin and dumping out any excess.)
2. Preheat the air fryer to 400°F.
3. Toss the mushrooms and asparagus in a bowl with the olive oil. Transfer the vegetables to the air fryer and air-fry for 7 minutes, shaking the basket once or twice to redistribute the Ingredients while they cook.
4. While the vegetables are cooking, make the soufflé base. Melt the butter in a saucepan on the stovetop over medium heat. Add the flour, stir and cook for a minute or two. Add the paprika, nutmeg, salt and pepper. Whisk in the milk and bring the mixture to a simmer to thicken. Remove the pan from the heat and add the cheese, stirring to melt. Let the mixture cool for just a few minutes and then whisk the egg yolks in, one at a time. Stir in the cooked mushrooms and asparagus. Let this soufflé base cool.
5. In a separate bowl, whisk the egg whites to soft peak stage (the point at which the whites can almost stand up on the end of your whisk). Fold the whipped egg whites into the soufflé base, adding a little at a time.
6. Preheat the air fryer to 330°F.
7. Transfer the batter carefully to the buttered ramekins, leaving about ½-inch at the top. Place the ramekins into the air fryer basket and air-fry for 14 minutes. The soufflés should have risen nicely and be brown on top. Serve immediately.

Eggplant Parmesan

Servings: 4

Cooking Time: 8 Minutes Per Batch

Ingredients:

- 1 medium eggplant, 6–8 inches long
- salt
- 1 large egg
- 1 tablespoon water
- ⅔ cup panko breadcrumbs
- ⅓ cup grated Parmesan cheese, plus more for serving
- 1 tablespoon Italian seasoning
- ¾ teaspoon oregano
- oil for misting or cooking spray
- 1 24-ounce jar marinara sauce
- 8 ounces spaghetti, cooked
- pepper

Directions:

1. Preheat air fryer to 390°F.
2. Leaving peel intact, cut eggplant into 8 round slices about ¾-inch thick. Salt to taste.
3. Beat egg and water in a shallow dish.
4. In another shallow dish, combine panko, Parmesan, Italian seasoning, and oregano.
5. Dip eggplant slices in egg wash and then crumbs, pressing lightly to coat.
6. Mist slices with oil or cooking spray.
7. Place 4 eggplant slices in air fryer basket and cook for 8 minutes, until brown and crispy.
8. While eggplant is cooking, heat marinara sauce.
9. Repeat step 7 to cook remaining eggplant slices.
10. To serve, place cooked spaghetti on plates and top with marinara and eggplant slices. At the table, pass extra Parmesan cheese and freshly ground black pepper.

FISH AND SEAFOOD RECIPES

Fish-in-chips

Servings:4

Cooking Time: 11 Minutes

Ingredients:

- 1 cup All-purpose flour or potato starch
- 2 Large egg(s), well beaten
- 1½ cups (6 ounces) Crushed plain potato chips, preferably thick-cut or ruffled (gluten-free, if a concern)
- 4 4-ounce skinless cod fillets

Directions:

1. Preheat the air fryer to 400°F.
2. Set up and fill three shallow soup plates or small pie plates on your counter: one for the flour, one for the beaten egg(s), and one for the crushed potato chips.
3. Dip a piece of cod in the flour, turning it to coat on all sides, even the ends and sides. Gently shake off any excess flour, then dip it in the beaten egg(s). Gently turn to coat it on all sides, then let any excess egg slip back into the rest. Set the fillet in the crushed potato chips and turn several times and onto all sides, pressing gently to coat the fish. Dip it back in the egg(s), coating all sides but taking care that the coating doesn't slip off; then dip it back in the potato chips for a thick, even coating. Set it aside and coat more fillets in the same way.
4. When the machine is at temperature, set the fillets in the basket with as much air space between them as possible. Air-fry undisturbed for 11 minutes, until golden brown and firm but not hard.
5. Use kitchen tongs to transfer the fillets to a wire rack. Cool for just a minute or two before serving.

Sweet Potato–wrapped Shrimp

Servings:3

Cooking Time: 6 Minutes

Ingredients:

- 24 Long spiralized sweet potato strands
- Olive oil spray
- ¼ teaspoon Garlic powder
- ¼ teaspoon Table salt
- Up to a ⅛ teaspoon Cayenne
- 12 Large shrimp (20–25 per pound), peeled and deveined

Directions:

1. Preheat the air fryer to 400°F.
2. Lay the spiralized sweet potato strands on a large swath of paper towels and straighten out the strands to long ropes. Coat them with olive oil spray, then sprinkle them with the garlic powder, salt, and cayenne.
3. Pick up 2 strands and wrap them around the center of a shrimp, with the ends tucked under what now becomes the bottom side of the shrimp. Continue wrapping the remainder of the shrimp.
4. Set the shrimp bottom side down in the basket with as much air space between them as possible. Air-fry undisturbed for 6 minutes, or until the sweet potato strands are crisp and the shrimp are pink and firm.
5. Use kitchen tongs to transfer the shrimp to a wire rack. Cool for only a minute or two before serving.

Super Crunchy Flounder Fillets

Servings:2

Cooking Time: 6 Minutes

Ingredients:

- ½ cup All-purpose flour or tapioca flour
- 1 Large egg white(s)
- 1 tablespoon Water
- ¾ teaspoon Table salt
- 1 cup Plain panko bread crumbs (gluten-free, if a concern)
- 2 4-ounce skinless flounder fillet(s)
- Vegetable oil spray

Directions:

1. Preheat the air fryer to 400°F.
2. Set up and fill three shallow soup plates or small pie plates on your counter: one for the flour; one for the egg white(s), beaten with the water and salt until foamy; and one for the bread crumbs.
3. Dip one fillet in the flour, turning it to coat both sides. Gently shake off any excess flour, then dip the fillet in the egg white mixture, turning it to coat. Let any excess egg white mixture slip back into the rest, then set the fish in the bread crumbs. Turn it several times, gently pressing it into the crumbs to create an even crust. Generously coat both sides of the fillet with vegetable oil spray. If necessary, set it aside and continue coating the remaining fillet(s) in the same way.
4. Set the fillet(s) in the basket. If working with more than one fillet, they should not touch, although they may be quite close together, depending on the basket's size. Air-fry undisturbed for 6 minutes, or until lightly browned and crunchy.
5. Use a nonstick-safe spatula to transfer the fillet(s) to a wire rack. Cool for only a minute or two before serving.

Shrimp Patties

Servings: 4

Cooking Time: 10 Minutes

Ingredients:

- ½ pound shelled and deveined raw shrimp
- ¼ cup chopped red bell pepper
- ¼ cup chopped green onion
- ¼ cup chopped celery
- 2 cups cooked sushi rice
- ½ teaspoon garlic powder
- ½ teaspoon Old Bay Seasoning
- ½ teaspoon salt
- 2 teaspoons Worcestershire sauce
- ½ cup plain breadcrumbs
- oil for misting or cooking spray

Directions:

1. Finely chop the shrimp. You can do this in a food processor, but it takes only a few pulses. Be careful not to overprocess into mush.
2. Place shrimp in a large bowl and add all other ingredients except the breadcrumbs and oil. Stir until well combined.
3. Preheat air fryer to 390°F.
4. Shape shrimp mixture into 8 patties, no more than ½-inch thick. Roll patties in breadcrumbs and mist with oil or cooking spray.
5. Place 4 shrimp patties in air fryer basket and cook at 390°F for 10 minutes, until shrimp cooks through and outside is crispy.
6. Repeat step 5 to cook remaining shrimp patties.

Fish Sticks For Kids

Servings: 8

Cooking Time: 6 Minutes

Ingredients:

- 8 ounces fish fillets (pollock or cod)
- salt (optional)
- ½ cup plain breadcrumbs
- oil for misting or cooking spray

Directions:

1. Cut fish fillets into "fingers" about ½ x 3 inches. Sprinkle with salt to taste, if desired.
2. Roll fish in breadcrumbs. Spray all sides with oil or cooking spray.
3. Place in air fryer basket in single layer and cook at 390°F for 6 minutes, until golden brown and crispy.

Sesame-crusted Tuna Steaks

Servings:3

Cooking Time: 10-13 Minutes

Ingredients:

- ½ cup Sesame seeds, preferably a blend of white and black
- 1½ tablespoons Toasted sesame oil
- 3 6-ounce skinless tuna steaks

Directions:

1. Preheat the air fryer to 400°F.
2. Pour the sesame seeds on a dinner plate. Use ½ tablespoon of the sesame oil as a rub on both sides and the edges of a tuna steak. Set it in the sesame seeds, then turn it several times, pressing gently, to create an even coating of the seeds, including around the steak's edge. Set aside and continue coating the remaining steak(s).
3. When the machine is at temperature, set the steaks in the basket with as much air space between them as possible. Air-fry undisturbed for 10 minutes for medium-rare (not USDA-approved), or 12 to 13 minutes for cooked through (USDA-approved).
4. Use a nonstick-safe spatula to transfer the steaks to serving plates. Serve hot.

Coconut Shrimp

Servings: 4

Cooking Time: 12 Minutes

Ingredients:

- 1 pound large shrimp (about 16 to 20), peeled and de-veined
- ½ cup flour
- salt and freshly ground black pepper
- 2 egg whites
- ½ cup fine breadcrumbs
- ½ cup shredded unsweetened coconut
- zest of one lime
- ½ teaspoon salt
- ⅛ to ¼ teaspoon ground cayenne pepper
- vegetable or canola oil
- sweet chili sauce or duck sauce (for serving)

Directions:

1. Set up a dredging station. Place the flour in a shallow dish and season well with salt and freshly ground black pepper. Whisk the egg whites in a second shallow dish. In a third shallow dish, combine the breadcrumbs, coconut, lime zest, salt and cayenne pepper.
2. Preheat the air fryer to 400°F.
3. Dredge each shrimp first in the flour, then dip it in the egg mixture, and finally press it into the breadcrumb-coconut mixture to coat all sides. Place the breaded shrimp on a plate or baking sheet and spray both sides with vegetable oil.
4. Air-fry the shrimp in two batches, being sure not to over-crowd the basket. Air-fry for 5 minutes, turning the shrimp over for the last minute or two. Repeat with the second batch of shrimp.
5. Lower the temperature of the air fryer to 340°F. Return the first batch of shrimp to the air fryer basket with the second batch and air-fry for an additional 2 minutes, just to re-heat everything.
6. Serve with sweet chili sauce, duck sauce or just eat them plain!

Lobster Tails With Lemon Garlic Butter

Servings: 2

Cooking Time: 5 Minutes

Ingredients:

- 4 ounces unsalted butter
- 1 tablespoon finely chopped lemon zest
- 1 clove garlic, thinly sliced
- 2 (6-ounce) lobster tails
- salt and freshly ground black pepper
- ½ cup white wine
- ½ lemon, sliced
- vegetable oil

Directions:

1. Start by making the lemon garlic butter. Combine the butter, lemon zest and garlic in a small saucepan. Melt and simmer the butter on the stovetop over the lowest possible heat while you prepare the lobster tails.
2. Prepare the lobster tails by cutting down the middle of the top of the shell. Crack the bottom shell by squeezing the sides of the lobster together so that you can access the lobster meat inside. Pull the lobster tail up out of the shell, but leave it attached at the base of the tail. Lay the lobster meat on top of the shell and season with salt and freshly ground black pepper. Pour a little of the lemon garlic butter on top of the lobster meat and transfer the lobster to the refrigerator so that the butter solidifies a little.
3. Pour the white wine into the air fryer drawer and add the lemon slices. Preheat the air fryer to 400°F for 5 minutes.
4. Transfer the lobster tails to the air fryer basket. Air-fry at 370° for 5 minutes, brushing more butter on halfway through cooking. (Add a minute or two if your lobster tail is more than 6-ounces.) Remove and serve with more butter for dipping or drizzling.

Perfect Soft-shelled Crabs

Servings:2

Cooking Time: 12 Minutes

Ingredients:

- ½ cup All-purpose flour
- 1 tablespoon Old Bay seasoning
- 1 Large egg(s), well beaten
- 1 cup (about 3 ounces) Ground oyster crackers
- 2 2½-ounce cleaned soft-shelled crab(s), about 4 inches across
- Vegetable oil spray

Directions:

1. Preheat the air fryer to 375°F (or 380°F or 390°F, if one of these is the closest setting).
2. Set up and fill three shallow soup plates or small pie plates on your counter: one for the flour, whisked with the Old Bay until well combined; one for the beaten egg(s); and one for the cracker crumbs.
3. Set a soft-shelled crab in the flour mixture and turn to coat evenly and well on all sides, even inside the legs. Dip the crab into the egg(s) and coat well, turning at least once, again getting some of the egg between the legs. Let any excess egg slip back into the rest, then set the crab in the cracker crumbs. Turn several times, pressing very gently to get the crab evenly coated with crumbs, even between the legs. Generously coat the crab on all sides with vegetable oil spray. Set it aside if you're making more than one and coat these in the same way.
4. Set the crab(s) in the basket with as much air space between them as possible. They may overlap slightly, particularly at the ends of their legs, depending on the basket's size. Air-fry undisturbed for 12 minutes, or until very crisp and golden brown. If the machine is at 390°F, the crabs may be done in only 10 minutes.
5. Use kitchen tongs to gently transfer the crab(s) to a wire rack. Cool for a couple of minutes before serving.

Buttery Lobster Tails

Servings:4

Cooking Time: 6 Minutes

Ingredients:

- 4 6- to 8-ounce shell-on raw lobster tails
- 2 tablespoons Butter, melted and cooled
- 1 teaspoon Lemon juice
- ½ teaspoon Finely grated lemon zest
- ½ teaspoon Garlic powder
- ½ teaspoon Table salt
- ½ teaspoon Ground black pepper

Directions:

1. Preheat the air fryer to 375°F .
2. To give the tails that restaurant look, you need to butterfly the meat. To do so, place a tail on a cutting board so that the shell is convex. Use kitchen shears to cut a line down the middle of the shell from the larger end to the smaller, cutting only the shell and not the meat below, and stopping before the back fins. Pry open the shell, leaving it intact. Use your clean fingers to separate the meat from the shell's sides and bottom, keeping it attached to the shell at the back near the fins. Pull the meat up and out of the shell through the cut line, laying the meat on top of the shell and closing the shell (as well as you can) under the meat. Make two equidistant cuts down the meat from the larger end to near the smaller end, each about ¼ inch deep, for the classic restaurant look on the plate. Repeat this procedure with the remaining tail(s).
3. Stir the butter, lemon juice, zest, garlic powder, salt, and pepper in a small bowl until well combined. Brush this mixture over the lobster meat set atop the shells.
4. When the machine is at temperature, place the tails shell side down in the basket with as much air space between them as possible. Air-fry undisturbed for 6 minutes, or until the lobster meat has pink streaks over it and is firm.
5. Use kitchen tongs to transfer the tails to a wire rack. Cool for only a minute or two before serving.

Salmon Puttanesca En Papillotte With Zucchini

Servings: 2

Cooking Time: 17 Minutes

Ingredients:

- 1 small zucchini, sliced into ¼-inch thick half moons
- 1 teaspoon olive oil
- salt and freshly ground black pepper
- 2 (5-ounce) salmon fillets
- 1 beefsteak tomato, chopped (about 1 cup)
- 1 tablespoon capers, rinsed
- 10 black olives, pitted and sliced
- 2 tablespoons dry vermouth or white wine 2 tablespoons butter
- ¼ cup chopped fresh basil, chopped

Directions:

1. Preheat the air fryer to 400°F.
2. Toss the zucchini with the olive oil, salt and freshly ground black pepper. Transfer the zucchini into the air fryer basket and air-fry for 5 minutes, shaking the basket once or twice during the cooking process.
3. Cut out 2 large rectangles of parchment paper – about 13-inches by 15-inches each. Divide the air-fried zucchini between the two pieces of parchment paper, placing the vegetables in the center of each rectangle.
4. Place a fillet of salmon on each pile of zucchini. Season the fish very well with salt and pepper. Toss the tomato, capers, olives and vermouth (or white wine) together in a bowl. Divide the tomato mixture between the two fish packages, placing it on top of the fish fillets and pouring any juice out of the bowl onto the fish. Top each fillet with a tablespoon of butter.
5. Fold up each parchment square. Bring two edges together and fold them over a few times, leaving some space above the fish. Twist the open sides together and upwards so they can serve as handles for the packet, but don't let them extend beyond the top of the air fryer basket.
6. Place the two packages into the air fryer and air-fry at 400°F for 12 minutes. The packages should be puffed up and slightly browned when fully cooked. Once cooked, let the fish sit in the parchment for 2 minutes.
7. Serve the fish in the parchment paper, or if desired, remove the parchment paper before serving. Garnish with a little fresh basil.

Blackened Catfish

Servings: 4

Cooking Time: 8 Minutes

Ingredients:

- 1 teaspoon paprika
- 1 teaspoon garlic powder
- 1 teaspoon onion powder
- 1 teaspoon ground dried thyme
- ½ teaspoon ground black pepper
- ⅛ teaspoon cayenne pepper
- ½ teaspoon dried oregano
- ⅛ teaspoon crushed red pepper flakes
- 1 pound catfish filets
- ½ teaspoon sea salt
- 2 tablespoons butter, melted
- 1 tablespoon extra-virgin olive oil
- 2 tablespoons chopped parsley
- 1 lemon, cut into wedges

Directions:

1. In a small bowl, stir together the paprika, garlic powder, onion powder, thyme, black pepper, cayenne pepper, oregano, and crushed red pepper flakes.
2. Pat the fish dry with paper towels. Season the filets with sea salt and then coat with the blackening seasoning.
3. In a small bowl, mix together the butter and olive oil and drizzle over the fish filets, flipping them to coat them fully.
4. Preheat the air fryer to 350°F.
5. Place the fish in the air fryer basket and cook for 8 minutes, checking the fish for doneness after 4 minutes. The fish will flake easily when cooked.
6. Remove the fish from the air fryer. Top with chopped parsley and serve with lemon wedges.

SANDWICHES AND BURGERS RECIPES

Eggplant Parmesan Subs

Servings: 2

Cooking Time: 13 Minutes

Ingredients:

- 4 Peeled eggplant slices (about ½ inch thick and 3 inches in diameter)
- Olive oil spray
- 2 tablespoons plus 2 teaspoons Jarred pizza sauce, any variety except creamy
- ¼ cup (about ⅔ ounce) Finely grated Parmesan cheese
- 2 Small, long soft rolls, such as hero, hoagie, or Italian sub rolls (gluten-free, if a concern), split open lengthwise

Directions:

1. Preheat the air fryer to 350°F .
2. When the machine is at temperature, coat both sides of the eggplant slices with olive oil spray. Set them in the basket in one layer and air-fry undisturbed for 10 minutes, until lightly browned and softened.
3. Increase the machine's temperature to 375°F (or 370°F, if that's the closest setting—unless the machine is already at 360°F, in which case leave it alone). Top each eggplant slice with 2 teaspoons pizza sauce, then 1 tablespoon cheese. Air-fry undisturbed for 2 minutes, or until the cheese has melted.
4. Use a nonstick-safe spatula, and perhaps a flatware fork for balance, to transfer the eggplant slices cheese side up to a cutting board. Set the roll(s) cut side down in the basket in one layer (working in batches as necessary) and air-fry undisturbed for 1 minute, to toast the rolls a bit and warm them up. Set 2 eggplant slices in each warm roll.

Black Bean Veggie Burgers

Servings: 3

Cooking Time: 10 Minutes

Ingredients:

- 1 cup Drained and rinsed canned black beans
- ⅓ cup Pecan pieces
- ⅓ cup Rolled oats (not quick-cooking or steel-cut; gluten-free, if a concern)
- 2 tablespoons (or 1 small egg) Pasteurized egg substitute, such as Egg Beaters (gluten-free, if a concern)
- 2 teaspoons Red ketchup-like chili sauce, such as Heinz
- ¼ teaspoon Ground cumin
- ¼ teaspoon Dried oregano
- ¼ teaspoon Table salt
- ¼ teaspoon Ground black pepper
- Olive oil
- Olive oil spray

Directions:

1. Preheat the air fryer to 400°F.
2. Put the beans, pecans, oats, egg substitute or egg, chili sauce, cumin, oregano, salt, and pepper in a food processor. Cover and process to a coarse paste that will hold its shape like sugar-cookie dough, adding olive oil in 1-teaspoon increments to get the mixture to blend smoothly. The amount of olive oil is actually dependent on the internal moisture content of the beans and the oats. Figure on about 1 tablespoon (three 1-teaspoon additions) for the smaller batch, with proportional increases for the other batches. A little too much olive oil can't hurt, but a dry paste will fall apart as it cooks and a far-too-wet paste will stick to the basket.
3. Scrape down and remove the blade. Using clean, wet hands, form the paste into two 4-inch patties for the small batch, three 4-inch patties for the medium, or four 4-inch patties for the large batch, setting them one by one on a cutting board. Generously coat both sides of the patties with olive oil spray.
4. Set them in the basket in one layer. Air-fry undisturbed for 10 minutes, or until lightly browned and crisp at the edges.
5. Use a nonstick-safe spatula, and perhaps a flatware fork for balance, to transfer the burgers to a wire rack. Cool for 5 minutes before serving.

Chicken Apple Brie Melt

Servings: 3

Cooking Time: 13 Minutes

Ingredients:

- 3 5- to 6-ounce boneless skinless chicken breasts
- Vegetable oil spray
- 1½ teaspoons Dried herbes de Provence
- 3 ounces Brie, rind removed, thinly sliced
- 6 Thin cored apple slices
- 3 French rolls (gluten-free, if a concern)
- 2 tablespoons Dijon mustard (gluten-free, if a concern)

Directions:

1. Preheat the air fryer to 375°F .
2. Lightly coat all sides of the chicken breasts with vegetable oil spray. Sprinkle the breasts evenly with the herbes de Provence.
3. When the machine is at temperature, set the breasts in the basket and air-fry undisturbed for 10 minutes.
4. Top the chicken breasts with the apple slices, then the cheese. Air-fry undisturbed for 2 minutes, or until the cheese is melty and bubbling.
5. Use a nonstick-safe spatula and kitchen tongs, for balance, to transfer the breasts to a cutting board. Set the rolls in the basket and air-fry for 1 minute to warm through. (Putting them in the machine without splitting them keeps the insides very soft while the outside gets a little crunchy.)
6. Transfer the rolls to the cutting board. Split them open lengthwise, then spread 1 teaspoon mustard on each cut side. Set a prepared chicken breast on the bottom of a roll and close with its top, repeating as necessary to make additional sandwiches. Serve warm.

Philly Cheesesteak Sandwiches

Servings: 3

Cooking Time: 9 Minutes

Ingredients:

- ¾ pound Shaved beef
- 1 tablespoon Worcestershire sauce (gluten-free, if a concern)
- ¼ teaspoon Garlic powder
- ¼ teaspoon Mild paprika
- 6 tablespoons (1½ ounces) Frozen bell pepper strips (do not thaw)
- 2 slices, broken into rings Very thin yellow or white medium onion slice(s)
- 6 ounces (6 to 8 slices) Provolone cheese slices
- 3 Long soft rolls such as hero, hoagie, or Italian sub rolls, or hot dog buns (gluten-free, if a concern), split open lengthwise

Directions:

1. Preheat the air fryer to 400°F.
2. When the machine is at temperature, spread the shaved beef in the basket, leaving a ½-inch perimeter around the meat for good air flow. Sprinkle the meat with the Worcestershire sauce, paprika, and garlic powder. Spread the peppers and onions on top of the meat.
3. Air-fry undisturbed for 6 minutes, or until cooked through. Set the cheese on top of the meat. Continue air-frying undisturbed for 3 minutes, or until the cheese has melted.
4. Use kitchen tongs to divide the meat and cheese layers in the basket between the rolls or buns. Serve hot.

Dijon Thyme Burgers

Servings: 3

Cooking Time: 18 Minutes

Ingredients:

- 1 pound lean ground beef
- ⅓ cup panko breadcrumbs
- ¼ cup finely chopped onion
- 3 tablespoons Dijon mustard
- 1 tablespoon chopped fresh thyme
- 4 teaspoons Worcestershire sauce
- 1 teaspoon salt
- freshly ground black pepper
- Topping (optional):
- 2 tablespoons Dijon mustard
- 1 tablespoon dark brown sugar
- 1 teaspoon Worcestershire sauce
- 4 ounces sliced Swiss cheese, optional

Directions:

1. Combine all the burger ingredients together in a large bowl and mix well. Divide the meat into 4 equal portions and then form the burgers, being careful not to over-handle the meat. One good way to do this is to throw the meat back and forth from one hand to another, packing the meat each time you catch it. Flatten the balls into patties, making an indentation in the center of each patty with your thumb (this will help it stay flat as it cooks) and flattening the sides of the burgers so that they will fit nicely into the air fryer basket.
2. Preheat the air fryer to 370°F.
3. If you don't have room for all four burgers, air-fry two or three burgers at a time for 8 minutes. Flip the burgers over and air-fry for another 6 minutes.
4. While the burgers are cooking combine the Dijon mustard, dark brown sugar, and Worcestershire sauce in a small bowl and mix well. This optional topping to the burgers really adds a boost of flavor at the end. Spread the Dijon topping evenly on each burger. If you cooked the burgers in batches, return the first batch to the cooker at this time – it's ok to place the fourth burger on top of the others in the center of the basket. Air-fry the burgers for another 3 minutes.
5. Finally, if desired, top each burger with a slice of Swiss cheese. Lower the air fryer temperature to 330°F and air-fry for another minute to melt the cheese. Serve the burgers on toasted brioche buns, dressed the way you like them.

Chili Cheese Dogs

Servings: 3

Cooking Time: 12 Minutes

Ingredients:

- ¾ pound Lean ground beef
- 1½ tablespoons Chile powder
- 1 cup plus 2 tablespoons Jarred sofrito
- 3 Hot dogs (gluten-free, if a concern)
- 3 Hot dog buns (gluten-free, if a concern), split open lengthwise
- 3 tablespoons Finely chopped scallion
- 9 tablespoons (a little more than 2 ounces) Shredded Cheddar cheese

Directions:

1. Crumble the ground beef into a medium or large saucepan set over medium heat. Brown well, stirring often to break up the clumps. Add the chile powder and cook for 30 seconds, stirring the whole time. Stir in the sofrito and bring to a simmer. Reduce the heat to low and simmer, stirring occasionally, for 5 minutes. Keep warm.
2. Preheat the air fryer to 400°F.
3. When the machine is at temperature, put the hot dogs in the basket and air-fry undisturbed for 10 minutes, or until the hot dogs are bubbling and blistered, even a little crisp.
4. Use kitchen tongs to put the hot dogs in the buns. Top each with a ½ cup of the ground beef mixture, 1 tablespoon of the minced scallion, and 3 tablespoons of the cheese. (The scallion should go under the cheese so it superheats and wilts a bit.) Set the filled hot dog buns in the basket and air-fry undisturbed for 2 minutes, or until the cheese has melted.
5. Remove the basket from the machine. Cool the chili cheese dogs in the basket for 5 minutes before serving.

White Bean Veggie Burgers

Servings: 3

Cooking Time: 13 Minutes

Ingredients:

- 1⅓ cups Drained and rinsed canned white beans
- 3 tablespoons Rolled oats (not quick-cooking or steel-cut; gluten-free, if a concern)
- 3 tablespoons Chopped walnuts
- 2 teaspoons Olive oil
- 2 teaspoons Lemon juice
- 1½ teaspoons Dijon mustard (gluten-free, if a concern)
- ¾ teaspoon Dried sage leaves
- ¼ teaspoon Table salt
- Olive oil spray
- 3 Whole-wheat buns or gluten-free whole-grain buns (if a concern), split open

Directions:

1. Preheat the air fryer to 400°F.
2. Place the beans, oats, walnuts, oil, lemon juice, mustard, sage, and salt in a food processor. Cover and process to make a coarse paste that will hold its shape, about like wet sugar-cookie dough, stopping the machine to scrape down the inside of the canister at least once.
3. Scrape down and remove the blade. With clean and wet hands, form the bean paste into two 4-inch patties for the small batch, three 4-inch patties for the medium, or four 4-inch patties for the large batch. Generously coat the patties on both sides with olive oil spray.
4. Set them in the basket with some space between them and air-fry undisturbed for 12 minutes, or until lightly brown and crisp at the edges. The tops of the burgers will feel firm to the touch.
5. Use a nonstick-safe spatula, and perhaps a flatware fork for balance, to transfer the burgers to a cutting board. Set the buns cut side down in the basket in one layer (working in batches as necessary) and air-fry undisturbed for 1 minute, to toast a bit and warm up. Serve the burgers warm in the buns.

www.ingramcontent.com/pod-product-compliance
Ingram Content Group UK Ltd.
Pitfield, Milton Keynes, MK11 3LW, UK
UKHW051132260726
13967UKWH00010B/3009

9 781803 200446